This Book Warps

SPACE
and
TIME

This Book Warps

SPACE
and
TIME

Selections from
The Journal of Irreproducible Results

Edited by Norman Sperling

**Andrews McMeel
Publishing, LLC**

Kansas City

08 09 10 11 12 WKT 10 9 8 7 6 5 4 3 2 1

ISBN-13: 978-0-7407-7713-4

ISBN-10: 0-7407-7713-0

Library of Congress Control Number: 2008921600

www.andrewsmcmeel.com

www.jir.com

ATTENTION: SCHOOLS AND BUSINESSES
Andrews McMeel books are available at quantity discounts with bulk purchase for educational, business, or sales promotional use. For information, please write to: Special Sales Department, Andrews McMeel Publishing, LLC, 1130 Walnut Street, Kansas City, Missouri 64106.

PRODUCT WARNING LABELS

Susan Hewitt and Edward Subitzky

As scientists and concerned citizens, we applaud the recent trend toward legislation that requires the prominent placing of warnings on products that present hazards to the public. Yet we must also offer the caution that such warnings, however well intentioned, merely scratch the surface of what is necessary in this important area. This is especially true in light of the findings of twentieth-century physics.

We are therefore proposing that, as responsible scientists, we join together in an intensive push for new laws that will mandate the conspicuous placement of suitably informative warnings on the packaging of every product offered for sale in the United States of America. Our list of suggested warnings follows.

WARNING:
This Product Warps Space
and Time in Its Vicinity.

COMPONENT EQUIVALENCY NOTICE:
The Subatomic Particles (Electrons, Protons, etc.) in This Product Are Exactly the Same in Every Measurable Respect as Those Used in the Products of Other Manufacturers, and No Claim to the Contrary May Legitimately Be Expressed or Implied.

IMPORTANT NOTICE TO PURCHASERS:
The Entire Physical Universe, Including This Product, May One Day Collapse Back into an Infinitesimally Small Space. Should Another Universe Subsequently Reemerge, the Existence of This Product in That Universe Cannot Be Guaranteed.

Newest rodeo category: **sending text messages from a bucking bronco.**

Dark-Suckers: The Age of Enlightenment Ends

Kirk R. Smith, University of California, Berkeley

There is no such thing as light. What there is in the Universe is dark. It is obvious from simple observations that this is so.

What we call light is merely the absence of dark. Dark is continually created. As fast as it is whisked away, more fills up the space.

We can easily establish these facts long hidden by the tenaciousness with which light-headed scientists have clung to their illuminating but less than brilliant theories.

What we have called sources of light are in reality dark-sinks. They are places into which dark is sucked. See Figure 1. More dark is created and is sucked into the "light." It flows at the speed of dark, of course, which is relatively fast.

It is often observed that "light bulbs," after failure, contain a quantity of dark inside. The dark has clogged them up. Normally, of course, the dark is sucked down the wires and into

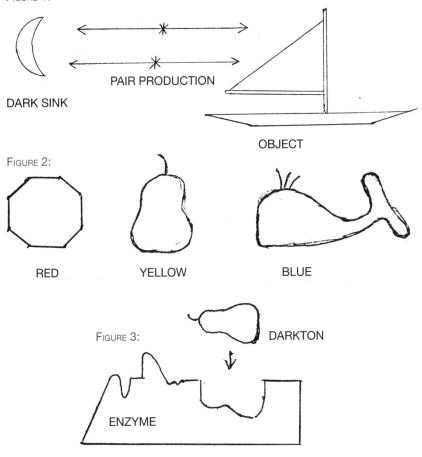

FIGURE 1:

DARK SINK

PAIR PRODUCTION

OBJECT

FIGURE 2:

RED   YELLOW   BLUE

FIGURE 3:   DARKTON

ENZYME

power stations, where it is put back into the world in the form of air and water dark (smoke and pollution).

A fire in the fireplace uses chemical energy to pull the dark out of the room, leaving a bucketful in the fireplace afterwards.

Shadows are created simply by objects being in the way. The dark can't get by on its way to the dark-sink.

I suspect that a physicist, being conservative by nature as well as by law, will not accept this radical new theory without flaring up.

Colors? Different-shaped darktons. See Figure 2 for the most probable shapes. We are able to see different colors because of these shapes. For example, when the newly created darkton is yellow in shape, it fits into the enzymes in our eyes, as in Figure 3. As we have seen in molecular biology texts, enzymes come in the appropriate designs to detect all possible color-shapes.

This is by no means a revelation to be treated lightly. Our view of the world will be markedly changed. "As the sunrise empties the valleys of dark" will become precise scientific description instead of poetic vision. Basic philosophy will have to be transformed. "Let there be dark-suck"? But first there had to be the dark. Perhaps we should alter the old adage, and, applying ourselves directly to the source, we should indeed curse the darkness.

Axioms

John F. Moffitt, PhD, Las Cruces, New Mexico

- The supply of truth always greatly exceeds its demand.
- The greatest obstacle to making intelligent decisions is human nature.
- The distinction between genius and stupidity is that the former has its limits.
- Ambition is a poor excuse for not having enough sense to be lazy.
- Whereas hard work is said to pay off in the future, laziness pays off now.
- If at first you don't succeed, then speedily destroy all evidence that you ever tried.
- The sooner you fall behind, the more time you'll have to catch up.
- If it's not one thing, it's two—or many more.
- Ignorance, particularly of how sausages and laws are made, has its advantages.
- Less is less. (Always.)

Real Questions from
Earth Science Students

Brenna Lorenz, Penn State University

- Are the rivers flowing up the mountain or down the mountain?

- Is that the ocean? (asked while on a field trip to Marine Lab Beach on Guam, a small island in the Pacific)

- How can the river be flowing north? That's uphill!

- How can mass wasting be an agent of landscape formation on the Moon? The Moon has no gravity!

- How do I get water into this beaker?

Coffee =

$Co(Fe)_2$

Fedspeak

William A. Voelkle

The primary purpose of Fedspeak is to inform the cognizant individual, and at the same time inject notes of chaos and utter incoherence into the ears of noncognizant personnel. Acronyms, the most versatile and powerful of all the Fedspeak tools, must be chosen and applied with great care. Interpretation by noninformed individuals would wreck security and demoralize the most efficient engineer, systems planner, or technical writer.

In no circumstances should an acronym be too similar to the actual message to be derived therefrom. For example, BOSS means Bio-Astronautic Orbiting Space Station; clearly this is a good acronym, as it is evident that anyone actually on a BOSS is not a boss. The classic bad example involves the Back-Up Guidance System (BUGS), which is easily susceptible to interpretation by anyone, realizing that indeed the system has its fair share of bugs.

Whenever possible, use at least two acronyms in conjunction to ensure maximum effectiveness and security.

For example, the sentence "Repair the Photo-Optical Recording Tracker of the Programmed Integrated Maintenance unit" should read "Repair the PORT PRISM." One can easily envision the improved clarity of this phrase over the standard.

RULES AND AXIOMS OF FEDSPEAK

- Acronymic efficiency increases as the cube of the number of letters in the acronym. Corollary: Whenever acronyms or abbreviations exceed four letters, suitable condensations thereof should be employed, using the same ground rules as in the formation of regular acronyms.
- At least two nonsimilar working definitions of each acronym should be employed frequently, distinguishable by arbitrary, prearranged physical signals that only the cognizant individuals, naturally, are aware of. This technique is especially useful in giving presentations.
- Whenever possible, use subordinate words or articles in the formation of acronyms.

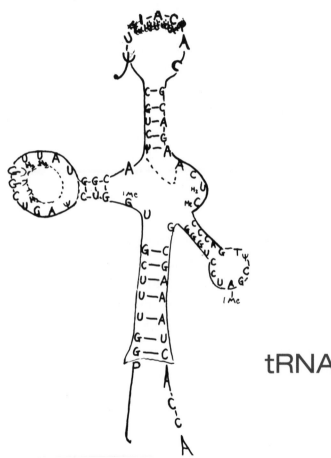

tRNA VALINE YEAST

THE BEARD-SECOND, A NEW UNIT OF LENGTH

Kemp Bennett Kolb

JUST AS ASTRONOMERS HAVE a cosmic unit of length related to the time something special travels at its own speed, physics has long awaited (1) a corresponding unit in the microcosmos. The proposed unit is the beard-second: the distance that a standard beard grows in one second. Conveniently, there are nearly 10^{24} beard seconds in one light year, placing the new unit in the virus particle range.

To complete the definition, a standard beard is defined as growing on a standard face at a rate of 1 beard-second (exactly 100 angstroms) per second.

---

1. Joe Slopnick, "I Am Waiting for a New Unit in the Microcosmos," *J. Things That Ought to Be Dn.,* 1492, 2, 69–94.

Do 1,000 chameleons make a chabeleon?

Risky Pleasures

Jim Eberhart,

University of Colorado at Colorado Springs

Many years ago I taught a course on personal and technological risk. It was at the beginning of the so-called safe sex campaign and also early in the worldwide HIV epidemic. One part of the course involved classroom work on a computer model to help in visualizing the risk of HIV transmission from protected and unprotected sex. We had good data on the risk of infection per encounter and also on the average frequency of sexual encounters. Medical studies placed the latter figure at twice per week. We decided to convert both our risk rate and encounter frequency to time units of days. That unit conversion gave us an average frequency of 2/7 of an encounter per day. As we all entered this fraction in one line of our BASIC code, one of my students exclaimed just loud enough to be heard, "Oh no, that would be too frustrating!"

PRODUCT WARNING LABELS

Susan Hewitt and Edward Subitzky

PUBLIC NOTICE AS REQUIRED BY LAW:
Any Use of This Product, in Any Manner Whatsoever,
Will Increase the Amount of Disorder in the
Universe. Although No Liability Is Implied Herein,
the Consumer Is Warned That This Process Will
Ultimately Lead to the Heat Death of the Universe.

NOTE:
The Most Fundamental Particles in This Product
Are Held Together by a "Gluing" Force About Which
Little Is Currently Known and Whose Adhesive Power
Therefore Cannot Be Permanently Guaranteed.

ATTENTION:
Despite Any Other Listing of Product Contents Found
Hereon, the Consumer Is Advised That, in Actuality, This
Product Consists of 99.9999999999% Empty Space.

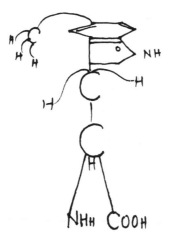

Methyl Tryptophan

Void Unless Good

Ralph A. Lewin

When we first moved and began to settle down, we needed curtains, among other things. We found a suitable
set of draperies in a large department store, J. C. Penney's, but
the saleswoman was reluctant to accept a personal check unless
we could establish our bona fides.

I offered her my driver's license—sorry, not acceptable.
My U.S. immigration card—not acceptable. My Social Security
card—not acceptable. In desperation, I handed her my wallet,
bulging with little else but cards, and asked her to see whether
she could find one that would assuage her doubts as to our
respectability.

She thumbed past memberships in the American Association
of University Professors, the United Nations Association, the
International Esperanto Association, and the San Diego Zoological
Society, and finally stopped at ID card number 576, whereon my
membership in the Society for Basic Irreproducible Research had
been certified by no less a personage than X. Perry Mental himself.

"This will do," said the discriminating lady with a satisfied smile. She accepted my check, copied details of my SBIR membership on its back, and slipped it under the cash drawer.

She packaged the curtains and bade us a sunny "good afternoon!" With what may have sounded like a choked sob of gratitude, I thanked the good lady, and we took the curtains home.

(We're pleased with the curtains, and there was nothing wrong with the check. This is an absolutely true story.)

Wacky Warning Labels

Robert B. Dorigo Jones,
Michigan Lawsuit Abuse Watch, www.mlaw.org

- A label on a baby stroller warns, "Remove child before folding."
- A brass fishing lure with a three-pronged hook on the end warns, "Harmful if swallowed."
- A household iron warns users, "Never iron clothes while they are being worn."
- A label on a hair dryer reads, "Never use hair dryer while sleeping."
- A warning on an electric drill made for carpenters cautions, "This product not intended for use as a dental drill."
- The label on a bottle of drain cleaner warns, "If you do not understand, or cannot read, all directions, cautions, and warnings, do not use this product."
- A smoke detector warns, "Do not use the Silence Feature in emergency situations. It will not extinguish a fire."

**If .com became .calm,
these would be choice domains:**

yoga.calm

cooland.calm

laidback.calm

relax.calm

CANDIDATE FOR A PULLET SURPRISE ——

Jerrold H. Zar, Northern Illinois University

I have a spelling checker,
It came with my PC.
It plane lee marks four my revue
Miss steaks aye can knot sea.

Eye ran this poem threw it,
Your sure reel glad two no.
Its vary polished in it's weigh.
My checker tolled me sew.

A checker is a bless sing,
It freeze yew lodes of thyme.
It helps me right awl stiles two reed,
And aides me when eye rime.

Each frays come posed up on my screen
Eye trussed too bee a joule.
The checker pours o'er every word
To cheque sum spelling rule.

Bee fore a veiling checker's
Hour spelling mite decline,
And if we're lacks oar have a laps,
We wood bee maid too wine.

Butt now bee cause my spelling
Is checked with such grate flare,
Their are know fault's with in my cite,
Of nun eye am a wear.

Now spelling does knot phase me,
It does knot bring a tier.
My pay purrs awl due glad den
With wrapped word's fare as hear.

To rite with care is quite a feet
Of witch won should bee proud,
And wee mussed dew the best wee can,
Sew flaw's are knot aloud.

Sow ewe can sea why aye dew prays
Such soft wear four pea seas,
And why eye brake in two averse
Buy righting want too pleas.

—Title suggested by Pamela Brown. Based on opening lines suggested by Mark Eckman. By the author's count, 127 of the 224 words of the poem are incorrect (although all words are correctly spelled).

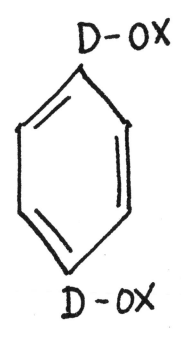

Paradox

THE STORY OF CREATION FOR THE MTV GENERATION

(Duration of needed attention span: 30 seconds)

Joel Kirschbaum, Institute for Motivated Behavior

IN THE BEGINNING, the creator first made a television set and, with a click of the on/off switch, separated the light from the dark.

On the TV set the creator showed pictures of suns, planets, and galaxies, but they drew a zero rating because there was no audience. So the creator started life from the dust and water of the planet Earth. Knowing that simple is better than complex, and thus good, the creator watched from above the evolution of the plants and animals and the creatures of the seas. On seeing the ponderous dinosaurs eventually produce tiny birds, and even the duck-billed platypus, the creator laughed pleasantly and thought, "Sometimes I surprise even myself."

The creator had an audience of but one person: Adam. After seeing that the solitary man had no one to talk to during the programming except the screen, he contrived him a companion, Eve. The first couple briefly examined the world and then concentrated on who should have the remote control, because the creator, while making all creatures two by two, had made only one TV set and controller.

One day, the serpent rolled an apple over the TV schedule, causing the R and X-rated programming to appear. Thus did Adam and Eve learn about sin.

MATHEMATICAL TERMS FOR SOCIAL DESCRIPTION

Henry Winthrop, University of South Florida

- **Almost periodic functions:** Useless meetings called almost regularly to bring organized confusion out of disorganized chaos.

- **Closed sets:** The locus of all mossbacks socially equidistant from a given mossback.

- **Coefficient of determination:** A faculty wife who makes all the major decisions about the ambitions of her professorial husband.

- **Combinatorial analysis:** The technique of deciding which faculty members would get along if appointed to the same committee.

- **Complex domain:** Any area of administrative decision that is difficult to understand because there are so many imaginary factors involved.

28

Occupational Safety and Health Administration:
A New Standard

Here's a pip, reported by the Consulting Engineers Council: OSHA has outdone itself in governmentalese.

They define the word *exit* as follows: "Exit is the portion of a means of egress which is separated from all other spaces of the building or structure by construction or equipment as required in this subpart to provide a protected way to travel to the exit discharge." They then had to define *exit discharge* as follows: "Exit discharge is that portion of a means of egress between the termination of an exit and a public way." Webster does it so much more easily; to him an exit is "a way out of an enclosed place or space."

Correction:
the Chinese vase described as a blue Ming deil was actually from Bloomingdale.

Pickles and Humbug:
A BIT OF COMPARATIVE LOGIC

Pickles will kill you! Every pickle you eat brings you nearer to death. Amazingly, the "thinking man" has failed to grasp the terrifying significance of the phrase "in a pickle." Although leading horticulturists have long known that *Cucumis sativus* possesses indehiscent pepos, the pickle industry continues to expand.

Pickles are associated with all major diseases of the body. Eating them breeds wars and Communism. They can be related to most airline tragedies. Auto accidents are caused by pickles. There is a positive relationship between crime waves and consumption of this fruit of the cucurbit family. For example,

- Nearly all sick people have eaten pickles. The effects are obviously cumulative.
- 99.9% of all people who die from cancer have eaten pickles.
- 100% of all soldiers have eaten pickles.
- 96.8% of all Red sympathizers have eaten pickles.

- 99.7% of the people involved in air and auto accidents ate pickles within fourteen days before the accident.
- 93.1% of juvenile delinquents come from homes where pickles are served frequently.

Evidence points to the long-term effects of pickle eating:
- Of the people born in 1839 who later dined on pickles, there has been a 100% mortality.
- All pickle eaters born between 1919 and 1929 have wrinkled skin, have lost most of their teeth, have brittle bones, and have failing eyesight—if the ills of eating pickles have not already caused their death.
- Even more convincing is the report of a noted team of medical specialists: Rats force-fed 20 pounds of pickles per day for thirty days developed bulging abdomens. Their appetites for wholesome food were destroyed.
- The only way to avoid the deleterious effects of pickle eating is to change eating habits. Eat orchid petal soup. Practically no one has problems from eating orchid petal soup.

Too Much Sodium

Brian Malow, www.butseriously.com

My sister recently told me that she won't eat Chinese food any more because it has too much sodium. But isn't that ridiculous? To single out one element from the periodic table? You'd have to have a pretty sensitive palate:

"Oh, I don't eat Mexican food, too much magnesium."

Or "Waiter, I'm sorry, I asked for the beryllium on the side."

Or "Nothing ruins a ham and cheese sandwich like a tad too much molybdenum."

How many times have you said that? Personally, I love Chinese food. I don't care if there's plutonium in it; it might be a little hot, but I'm eating it.

—John Chase, www.chasetoons.com,
www.cafepress.com/chasetoons

Technological Anglo-Saxon Polysyllabic Ornamentation

Gerald Basset

It might be anticipated that at professorial alignment there would be disapprobation of the employment of circumlocutory terminology. There is "Why the **** doesn't the *** *** say what he means?" In the relationship of the majority of the scientific and technological intelligentsia, conversation may have a tendency to be colloquial: "Tell the *** *** not to be such a *** ***."

It is interesting to observe, however, that the intellectual development of intelligent individuals, elevated by their educational attainments, encourages polysyllabic ornamentation of their scriptural assertions. The characteristic action of expressible divulgations in the systematization of communication, utilizing the typographical reproduction of linguistic interpretation, frequently encourages the transliteration of unintelligible representation, and the perspicacity of technologists may be overwhelmed by psychologically inundating superfluities, thus producing a conglomeration of sociological denominations intercommunicating at ideological, interlingual, intercontinental magnitudes.

Axioms

John F. Moffitt, PhD, Las Cruces, New Mexico

- Friends may come and go, but enemies will always accumulate.
- I intend to live forever. So far, so good.
- The colder the X-ray table, the more of your body is required to be on it.
- To stay healthy, you must: a) Eat and drink what you abhor. b) Do what you'd rather not.
- If it tastes good, it's trying to kill you.
- The hardness of the butter is proportional to the softness of the bread.
- The early bird may get the worm, but the *second* mouse gets the cheese.
- Eagles may soar, but weasels don't get sucked into jet engines.
- Economists' presumptions are as valid as yours: bad.
- 99% of lawyers give the rest a bad name.

Project Management Vocabulary

B. Sparks, Consulting Engineer

A Project: An assignment that can't be completed by either walking across the hall or making one telephone call.

To Activate a Project: To make additional copies and add to the distribution list.

To Implement a Project: To acquire all the physical space available and assign responsibilities to anyone in sight.

Consultant (or Expert): Anyone more than 50 miles from home.

Coordinator: The person who really doesn't know what's going on.

Channels: The people you wouldn't see or write to if your life depended on it.

Expedite: To contribute to the present chaos.

Conference (or Meeting): The activity that brings
all work and progress to a standstill.

Negotiating: Shouting demands, interspersed with gnashing teeth.

Re-Orientation: Starting to work again.

Making a Survey: Most of the personnel are on a boondoggle.

Under Consideration: Never heard of it.

Under Active Consideration: The memo is lost and is being looked for.

Will Be Looked Into: Maybe the whole thing
will be forgotten by the next meeting.

Reliable Source: The guy you just met.

Informed Source: The guy who introduced you.

Unimpeachable Source: The guy who started the rumor.

Read and Initial: To spread the responsibility
in case everything goes wrong.

The Other Viewpoint: Let them get it off
their chest so they'll shut up.

Clarification: Muddy the water so they can't see bottom.

See Me Later on This: I am as confused as you are.

Will Advise You in Due Course: When
we figure it out, we'll tell you.

In Process: Trying to get through the paper mill.

Modification: A complete redesign.

Orientation: Confusing a new member of the project.

Reorganization: Assigning someone new to save the project.

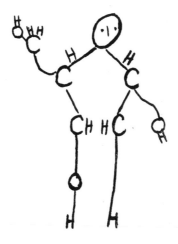

Desoxyribose

I bought the most powerful universal remote control. I hit "Rewind," and the Universe started to contract.

—Comedian Norm Goldblatt, www.normgoldblatt.com

JAMES BOND IN SOUTH INDIA

Pradeep Akkunoor, Pune, India

We South Indians usually have long names. In fact, until some years ago, the names used to give a complete history of the person. The name would include the person's father's name, his caste name, his village name, his grandfather's name, the family name, and, of course, his own given name. This illustration is often told:

Imagine the character James Bond, with his peculiar style of introducing himself by first saying "Bond," followed by a great smile and finally "James Bond." His style is absolutely killing, but he doesn't know the consequences when he meets our guy from South India.

JAMES BOND: "My name's Bond. [smiles and then says] James Bond. And you?"

THE SOUTH INDIAN GUY SHAKES HIS HAND AND REPLIES:
"I am Sai.

Venkata Sai.

Siva Venkata Sai.

Laxminarayana Siva Venkata Sai.

Srinivasulu Laxminarayana Siva Venkata Sai.

Rajasekhara Srinivasulu Laxminarayana Siva Venkata
Sai.

Sitaramanjaneyulu Rajasekhara Srinivasulu
Laxminarayana Siva Venkata Sai.

Bommiraju Sitaramanjaneyulu Rajasekhara Srinivasulu
Laxminarayana Siva Venkata Sai."

Sabotaged Bubblewrap!

Lou Lippman, Western Washington University

Preliminary intelligence indicates that a plastics plant in a remote country, where supervision is lax, has exported more than 100,000 bolts of plastic packing materials to the United States since June 2004. This packing material consists of air-filled plastic impact cushioning pockets often called bubblewrap or bubble packing by the general public.

Taking advantage of the lack of controls, suspected terrorists have contaminated the bubbles with either some type of biological agent (perhaps spores) or a gas that induces swelling and itching, red eye, and acute respiratory agitation. This form of red eye cannot be cured by even the most advanced cameras.

The terrorists involved in the manufacture of this product are well aware that Americans have an uncontrollable urge to manipulate the wrapping after use, popping the little bubbles. Therefore, this is an excellent delivery mechanism for causing widespread and random exposure of the American public to harmful substances. Citizens should take care to keep the bubblewrap intact when removing items from shipping cartons, and to keep it away from children, who have an especially difficult time resisting the urge to jump on it and pop the bubbles.

Pentagon spokesofficer Dr. Amy Silvester stated, "These terrorists will stop at nothing to harm the American public. The intelligence necessary to know that these materials would be sent to America suggests an organized, well-funded consortium of terrorists. This strange pursuit of harming the American public has not been seen since the height of the Cold War." Victims exposed to the harmful substances should immediately seek medical attention.

Axioms

John F. Moffitt, PhD, Las Cruces, New Mexico

- One can always succeed at giving up.
- Optimists include anyone innocent of experience.
- Experience is something you don't get until just after you need it.
- Optimists proclaim that we live in the best of all possible worlds; pessimists know this to be a fact.
- True pessimism doubts even the sincerity of its own pessimism.
- It is always darkest just before it goes pitch black.
- Money may come and go. Debts, however, will always accumulate.
- Borrow money only from pessimists; they don't expect it back.
- Why do psychics have to ask you for your name?
- All those who believe in psychokinesis, please raise my hand.

Nutrition Facts

Karl Petruso, University of Texas at Arlington

Serving size 60 KB (approximately 2 minutes)

Servings per site 30

Calories 0   Calories from Fat 0

	% Daily Value*
Total Irony 500g	1,000%
Saturated irony 100g	200%
Polyunsaturated irony 250g	500%
Monounsaturated irony 150g	300%
Cholesterol 0mg	0%
Sodium 0g	0%
Total Bad Humors	1,200%
Choler 35mg	350%
Vitriol 5mg	50%
Phlegm 13mg	200%
Melancholy 10mg	100%
Other Humors and Vapors	800%
Spleen 12g	250%
Ennui 100mg	300%
Bile 20mg	100%
Smarm 0mg	0%
Irascibility 18g	250%
Protein 0g	0%
Puckishness 25g	400%
Calcium 0g	0%
Crankiness 60g	300%
Vitamin A 0g	0%
Pomposity 300mg	150%

*Percent Daily Values are based on a 2,000 calorie diet. Your daily needs may be higher if you have a gratuitously sunny weltanschauung.

Publisher commits an ordinal sin:
Developmental Dyslexia,
3nd Edition
Michael Thomson

—John Wiley & Sons Web site

SPORTING CURVES

Jack Paolin, Idea Lab, Inc.

The Hockey Stick Theory of Global Warming

1992 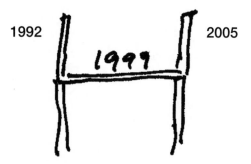 2005

1999

The Goalpost Theory of the National Deficit

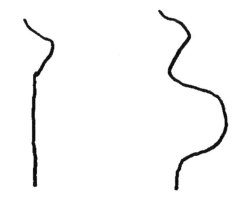

The Basketball Theory of Pro-Choice

The Baseball Bat Theory of Oversimplification

Objective: To fulfill all the tasks assigned and tend to learn to get succeeded in the entire future prospectus.

—From the résumé of an unsuccessful job seeker

The Gremlin

Glenn Johnson, MD, Orthopedic Surgery Editor

An elderly patient said he thought he had a "gremlin gnawing away inside, causing pain" in his left shoulder. This photo is four or five slices in, on the anteroposterior MRI scan. I ended up doing surgery and found that he had a massive rotator cuff tear. He's doing superbly well now. Moral of the story: Believe what patients tell you!

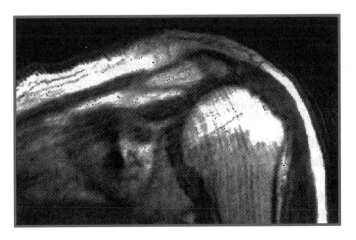

Demeter was the goddess of the metric system.

Physician Participation

Christopher Johnston

There is a definite trend to include physicians more actively in the daily operations of hospitals. Compelled by the desire to be one of the first, at our hospital we encourage physicians to participate in daily problems.

To share our experiences, the following represents our very first efforts. It is hoped that it will prove helpful to those who follow.

CLEANING THE O.R. FLOOR

Will Sliceum, MD

Preliminary Note: Preliminary examinations showed the subject to be a well nourished, eight-year-old, white asphalt tile floor. Light reflection and color were within normal limits, and there appeared to be no marked degree of subepithelial edema.

Wallboards, kick plates, and floor mats were all within normal limits. However, the anterior mat demonstrated a cicatrix that appeared to have been closed with two interrupted 5-0 silk sutures. Posterior corridor door revealed a scotoma, emesis, and some degree of lithiasis.

Findings and Procedures: After satisfactory restriction of traffic was obtained, the floor, in the supine position, was prepped with Ioprep. A swab application was made from the left ventral area to the dorsal exterior. The original application was extended somewhat laterally. The floor was then examined. The proximal and distal ends of the area were identified and irrigated with saline solution.

Attention was then turned to repair of two lacerations. The repair was done using #2 Tevdek. After cut ends had been freshened with a razor blade, approximately eight to ten interrupted sutures were needed to repair the median laceration using 6-0 interrupted sutures through the sheath of the tile. Following repair of the portion of the adjoining tile that had been damaged, the laceration was closed with heavy-gauge wire.

Dry sterile wax dressing was applied to the entire area. The floor tolerated the procedure well and was returned to public use in satisfactory condition.

Cat-ions

PRODUCT WARNING LABELS

Susan Hewitt and Edward Subitzky

WARNING:

This Product Attracts Every Other Piece of Matter in the
Universe, Including the Products of Other Manufacturers, with a
Force Proportional to the Product of the Masses and Inversely
Proportional to the Square of the Distance Between Them.

CAUTION:

The Mass of This Product Contains the Energy Equivalent
of 85 Million Tons of TNT per Net Ounce of Weight.

HANDLE WITH EXTREME CARE:

This Product Contains Minute Electrically Charged Particles
Moving at Velocities Greater Than 500 Million Miles per Hour.

CONSUMER NOTICE:

Because of the Uncertainty Principle, It Is Impossible for
the Consumer to Find Out at the Same Time Both Precisely
Where This Product Is and How Fast It Is Moving.

Unexplored Geological Epochs

Full of missing links: **Wouldacene**

Disproves evolution: **Nevercene**

Where the in-crowd digs: **Makethecene**

On a New Power Source

F. G. Hawksworth

With ever-increasing demands for power, a surprising, completely untapped power source exists throughout the West. Why not harness the explosive power of the fruit of the ubiquitous dwarf mistletoes (*Arceuthobium* spp.) of western conifers? These parasites have long been known (1,2), but their potential importance as a power source has not been recognized. Each dwarf mistletoe fruit contains a single projectile-like seed (about 1/10 of an inch long), which at maturity is ejected at speeds of about 90 feet per second (3,4).

Much potential energy is now being lost through wasteful seed dispersal. For example, just in Arizona and New Mexico, ponderosa pine dwarf mistletoe occurs on 2.5×10^6 acres (1). Estimated mistletoe production (3) averages about 25×10^4 seeds per acre. Thus approximately 6×10^{11} mistletoe seeds are produced annually just in the ponderosa pine type. Estimates of the force of the seeds based on their weight (2.7×10^{-3} grams) and velocity (2,740 cm/sec) indicate that each develops

8×10^{-8} horsepower. Multiply by the number of seeds produced to get 48×10^3 horsepower or (among friends) 50,000. Converted to more conventional terms, this represents 67,000 kilowatts!

It should be kept in mind that this is the potential of only one part of the West. Vast additional sources exist in mistletoe-infected pine, fir, larch, and hemlock forests throughout the West.

Development of this resource faces some slight difficulties, but none are insurmountable. Harnessing the power of billions of tiny fruits scattered over millions of acres represents a problem, and the energy must be harnessed during about 2×10^{-4} seconds when seed ejection occurs. Another minor handicap is that this power source is available only during the two or three weeks of seed dispersal. But typical American ingenuity and know-how, and a multi–billion-dollar crash program, could develop spectacular results.

Harnessing this power source would have many national advantages.

- It would enable us to beat the Russians at another game because their mistletoe power resources are extremely puny compared with ours.

- Directing seed power to more useful purposes than nature's debilitation of our forests should enhance our trees' sense of well-being.
- It would negate the need for additional Colorado River dams.

1. Andrews, S. R., and Daniels, J. P. 1960. *A Survey of Dwarf Mistletoes in Arizona and New Mexico.* U.S. Forest Service, Rocky Mtn. Station, Sta. Paper 49, 17p.

2. Gill, L. S. 1935. "*Arceuthobium* in the United States," *Trans. Conn. Acad. Arts & Sci.,* 32, 111–245.

3. Hawksworth, F. G. 1965. "Life Tables for Two Species of Dwarf Mistletoes. 1. Seed Dispersal, Interception and Movement," *Forest Science,* 11, 142–151.

4. Hinds, T. E., and Hawksworth, F. G. 1965. "Seed Dispersal Velocity in Four Dwarf Mistletoes," *Science,* 148, 517–519.

I keep hearing about inorganic chemists, but every chemist I've ever met is organic.

Testing Military Electronics

H. K. Mann

My work passes or fails the electromagnetic attributes of defense electronics for a country that need not be named.

Because of the sensitivity of electromagnetic radiation to boundary conditions, which (for a complex electronic system in a shielded room) includes the physical placement of anything in the room, the repeatability of results, for no apparent reason, is sometimes atrocious. At the worst, depending on the ability of the team running any particular test, the data are beyond useless.

In its infinite wisdom, management occasionally seizes on the most bizarre data (disclosed by undisclosed squealers) to derive any number of astounding conclusions, like the following:

- You're incompetent.
- Your test team is incompetent.
- Your test equipment is no good.

- Your setup is no good.
- Who cares, nobody ever passes these things anyway.
- And the classic: I don't care what the data say, the system passes!

If .org became .ore, these would be choice domains:

portland.ore eugene.ore coosbay.ore

iron.ore silver.ore

copper.ore

"THE TROUBLE, OF COURSE, IS THAT ALL THE IMPORTANT DISCOVERIES HAVE ALREADY BEEN MADE."

A Note on Matrix Theory

S. Kaplan

During the last seminar, a discussion arose over whether the term "positive semi-definite matrix" (that is, a matrix A for which $x^T A x \geq 0$ for all x) should be understood to include positive definite matrices (those for which $x^T A x > 0$ for all x), or whether it should be understood to mean that there does exist a nonzero x such that $x^T A x = 0$. Reference to Wachspress's *Iterative Solution of Elliptic Systems* (1966) shows that the latter understanding is the customary one. Thus, a positive semi-definite matrix is singular and hence definitely not positive definite.

If the positive semi-definite is to be understood in this limited sense, one may ask whether there is a term for the combined class of positive definite and positive semi-definite matrices. It would certainly seem appropriate to call a matrix in this combined class a "non-negative definite" matrix. However, such a matrix must be carefully distinguished from a "not-negative definite matrix" and from a "definite non-negative matrix." For although a definite non-negative matrix must be non-negative definite, a non-negative definite matrix is certainly not negative definite, so it is clear that a not-negative definite matrix may definitely be not non-negative definite.

This leads us naturally to a discussion of the properties of matrices that are definitely not non-negative definite. A matrix that is definitely not non-negative definite may, as we have seen, be negative definite, but it may also be not negative definite. Also, if a matrix is definitely not non-negative definite, then it is definitely not positive definite. However, it may be positive (that is, all the elements of the matrix are positive), for a positive matrix may be either non-negative definite or not non-negative definite. The only thing one can say about a positive matrix is that it positively may never be negative definite. A not-non-positive matrix may be positive definite, negative definite, non-negative definite, or none of these. The same is true about a not negative matrix. This brings us to our final theorem: A negative matrix is definitely not non-negative definite.

This theorem is best proven by the method of contradiction. (We leave it as an exercise.)

tRNA SERINE (RAT)

"Medical studies indicate
most people suffer a 68% hearing
loss when naked."

—Submitted by Richard D. Stacy

Apparently cited from Scheitel, S., Boland, B., Wollan, P., & Silverstein, M. "Agreement About Medical Diagnoses and Cardiovascular Risk Factors in the Ambulatory General Medical Examination." *Mayo Clinic Proceedings,* December 1996: 71(12); 1131–1137.

Mathematically speaking, it seems plain that "snakes on a plane" shouldn't be so dangerous. A plane is a flat geometric surface, so snakes confined to a plane would be unable to jump out of the plane and bite anyone who simply keeps their feet a little bit above the plane of the floor.

—Larry Lesser

THE RESOURCERER

A song by Ralph A. Lewin

I'm director of General Dæmonics,
A multifactorial show.
We revel in high electronics,
And systems that gurgle and glow.
From common electrical sockets
And gadgets that tinkle and blink,
We range into radar and rockets
And subjects too secret to think.

We're wizards at mine and munition;
We're wonders at thunderous rays
That sizzle a chap to perdition
In all sorts of horrible ways.
We push back the frontiers of science,
Refining a dust from the dust
For visiting death and defiance
On people we tend to distrust.

We've strings at the highest of levels,
Wherever ambition aspires:
Like all influential devils,
We have irons in dozens of fires.
Our salary scales are terrific,
And subject to weekly increase.
We peddle across the Pacific
All manner of matters but peace.

And now we're at work on a missile
For shooting a team into space
In search of an atom so fissile
It'll wipe out the rest of the race.

So three cheers for General Dæmonics
And all who fall under our spell.
Let nothing be slower than sonics,
And everything hotter than. . . .

[There is a searing flash and a super-sonic bang. In the purple afterglow, a
few mesons spin slowly across the stage and sink out of view.]

The latest postage increase seems to have paid for ware-housing, so they can store the mail longer before delivering it.

Most people think "Bill" in "Bill Gates" is short for "William." Actually, it's short for "Billion."

POPULAR LAWS OF PHYSICS WHERE **LOVE** REPLACES LIGHT OR MATTER

Jason Bennett and Sadie Dingfelder

♥ Although Einstein was famous for saying, "God does not play dice," he did not take into account the behavior of love at very small distances.

♥ Scientists have confirmed that the shape of our love is a saddle, not a parabola or Cartesian plane. Our love will expand outward forever.

♥ The leftover love from the big bang is called cosmic background love.

♥ A being of pure love would not experience time.

SMART APPLIANCES

YOUR MEATLOAF IS FINISHED!

SMART-ASS APPLIANCES

HEY, BOZO!! C'MERE AN' GIT YER TOAST 'FER IT GITS COLD!!

©R.FREED 2002

In My Statistics Course

Jim Vanderplas

I was trying to illustrate a three-dimensional analysis of variance design with a free-hand isometric drawing in graph-like form. Just as I was about to finish the drawing, I heard several students laughing loudly. I turned and asked what the joke was. One of the students confessed, "I think I'd prefer a thousand words."

MURPHY'S LAW AND A LIQUID HELIUM BATH TEMPERATURE CONTROLLER

C. M. Venegas, University of Colorado

A common mistake in feedback and control systems is to have a phase or polarity reversal of the feedback loop. This, of course, means that the feedback loop is unstable and will not be able to control. Because there are only two possible states of feedback polarity (positive and negative), the probability of having the correct polarity is 1:2. However, it is the considered opinion of many experimentalists that phasing errors occur much more often than half of the time. But this is only speculation because accurate statistics have not been tabulated (many of these phasing errors are never reported, quite understandably).

To avoid this difficulty, the loop phasing of our temperature controller was checked and rechecked on numerous occasions. Therefore, when it failed to control the temperature of a helium bath on its first test, a loop phasing error was not suspected. However, repeated attempts to control gave the same result: An increase in bath temperature produced an increase in output current to the bath heater. Various ingenious theories were proposed to explain the failure. However, subsequent investigation eliminated all but the following theory.

This is based on Murphy's Law: "If anything can go wrong, it will." Starting with this premise, we were able to build a convincing argument to the effect that, despite the checking and rechecking, we had actually succeeded in reversing the control loop phasing. Needless to say, this theory explains the experimental results completely.

If one then considers the mechanisms whereby control loop phasing is changed from correct to probably incorrect, one can only assume that human intervention plays a most important part in this process. Thus, humans are the chief propagators of Murphy's Law, although so far we have been unable to prove it conclusively.

Since 1970 I have taught about black holes and the singularities they are centered on. I don't recall anybody misspelling *singularity* until 2006. Thanks to powerful advertising about cellular telephones, several students then spelled it *cingularity*.

—Norman Sperling

Why My Cat is My CEO

Attilla Danko, cleardarksky.com

She:

- is either nowhere to be found or pesteringly domineering.
- wants attention *right now*.
- chases invisible things.
- sleeps while I work.
- never produces anything useful.
- expects me to clean up what she does produce.
- is the darling of visitors.
- can get me to do her bidding any time.

That's pretty much what I associate with CEOs.

A lot
of the
world
seems
to run
on *dork*
energy.

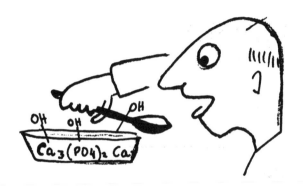

Hydroxy-appatite

Stand Up Straight

Brian Malow, www.butseriously.com

My mother used to tell me to "stand up straight." It was one of her favorite things to say: "Stand up straight!" Many other people also grew up hearing that phrase, I have discovered. It's nearly universal. As if mothers were programmed to say it.

In fact, I believe mothers have been telling their children to "stand up straight" longer than we realize—perhaps even to prehuman days.

What if that were the driving force behind the evolutionary trend to walk erect: mothers nagging their children up the evolutionary ladder?

"Stand up straight!"

"Don't drag your knuckles when you walk!"

"Were you born in a tree?"

"You want the other families to think we're not evolving?"

"No, Mom."

"Then how many times do I have to tell you?"

And therein lies the origin of mathematics: "How many times? Well, if I put the 3 here and carry the 1. . . ."

Our import business features many new shipments arriving:

- Contemporary Canadian wares from Canadia

- Exciting European styles from Europea

- Peruvian handicrafts from Peruvia

TOTAL IMMERSION GEOLOGISTS

Brenna Lorenz, Pennsylvania State University

ARE YOU TOTALLY OBSESSED with geology? If so, then you are a total immersion geologist. Here are the ten warning signs:

- You judge a restaurant by the type of decorative building stone they use, rather than their food.

- You manage to turn any conversation into a discussion of geology, as in "What did you think of that Super Bowl game last night?" "I must have missed that conference. Who sponsored it? Geological Society of America?"

- The only thing you notice about attractive people is the stones in their jewelry.

- You refuse to let nightfall stop your field excursions, and you continue looking at the outcrops using the headlights of your field vehicle.

- You like rock music only because it's called "rock" music.

- You will try to claw through the water flowing in a stream to get a better look at the bedrock at the base of the channel.

- You will walk across eight lanes of freeway traffic to see whether the outcrop on the other side is the same type of rock as the side you're parked on.

- You name your children after rocks and minerals.

- You're not sure whether you have children.

- You view nongeologists as subhuman.

If **.com** became **.cow**, these would be choice domains:

jersey.cow	holstein.cow	calf.cow
cash.cow	steer.cow	bull.cow

MORE
MATHEMATICAL TERMS
FOR SOCIAL DESCRIPTION
Henry Winthrop, University of South Florida

- **Confidence interval:** The hopeful waiting period before a request is turned down.

- **Correlation:** A person who discovers he or she shares your views shortly after you become part of the administration.

- **Covariance:** The usual academic phenomenon in which A goes along with whatever B says, particularly if B is the chairman.

- **Harmonic mean:** The ineffective and meaningless compromise that results from pooling the conflicting decisions of any number of ambitious characters.

- **Index of productivity:** A measure of both the quantity and the quality of one's remarks in committees.

Banana =

$Ba(Na)_2$

The government has revised the Food Guide Pyramid because not enough people are paying attention to it. Of course not. Nobody pays attention to pyramids. If they want us to pay attention, they should make it a Food Guide Pie Chart.

—Comedian Shaun Eli Breidbart, www.BrainChampagne.com

Officer: Do you know how fast you were going?

Me: Why, yes. I know exactly how fast I was going, but I'm completely lost.

Officer: Well, I'm going to let you off with a warning.

Me: Thanks a lot, Officer [twisting head to get a better look at badge] Heisenberg.

—Comedian Norm Goldblatt, www.normgoldblatt.com

Problem Solving

Jim Eberhart,

University of Colorado at Colorado Springs

I occasionally teach a mathematics course for liberal arts students. One day we were reviewing the concepts of ratios and percentages. I always try to use examples that the students can relate to, so I told them about how the majority of college students used to be men, but that now women are in the majority. Thus the ratio of men to women has changed from greater than 1 to less than 1 in recent years. Trying to bring a little humor to the discussion, I mentioned that this change has created a problem for women: the problem of where all the intelligent women are going to find intelligent men to marry. I had among my students a Mormon husband and wife. He raised his hand and told the class that the problem had a very simple solution: polygamy. I can only wonder what the pillow talk was like in their home that night!

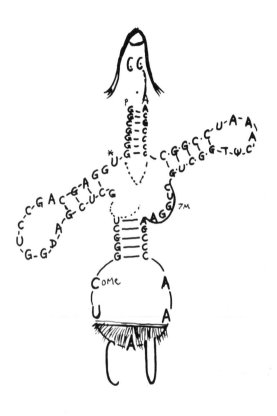

tRNA$_F^{METH}$

(E. coli)

97

Dog Blog

Peter Wilson

Scientists now say the dog invented the blog. Dr. Dean E. Roset and his team at the Canine Research and Physiology Institute are publishing results in the May–December issue of the *Journal of Animal Communication and Knowledge* that support the astounding claim.

"This was a multidisciplinary breakthrough," said Dr. Roset. "It took the combined expertise of body language professionals, MRI scanners, and even pet psychics to tease out this finding."

What the researchers found is that when dogs lift their legs, they are not saying, "This fire hydrant is mine." In other words, they are not marking territory, as animal behavior specialists previously assumed. What dogs are actually doing is leaving a pheromonally encoded message, which may be decoded later by other dogs with their highly acute olfactory sense. Dogs that later happen upon the message can read it, then post their own message in the same space. In short, dogs are blogging, not marking.

As to what exactly dogs are blogging about, "Dog only knows—I mean, God only knows," quipped Dr. Roset. But apparently there is more to it than "this is mine." Further research will be needed to decipher the messages, which are "more difficult to read than Egyptian hieroglyphics," according to Roset. Progress will depend on the level of funding that can be maintained in this vital area of research.

In an accompanying editorial, by Bell Thumper of the Intelligent Design Is Obviously True Institute Coalition, it is pointed out that the research supports Ecclesiastes 1:10: "Is there anything that can be called 'new'?" The institute promotes dialog between religion and science, and funds independent biblical science, according to a press statement. Thumper was not involved in the research.

Wacky Warning Labels

Robert B. Dorigo Jones,

Michigan Lawsuit Abuse Watch, www.mlaw.org

- A can of self-defense pepper spray warns users, "May irritate eyes."
- A warning on a pair of shin guards manufactured for bicyclists says, "Shin pads cannot protect any part of the body they do not cover."
- A snowblower warns, "Do not use snowblower on roof."
- A dishwasher carries this warning: "Do not allow children to play in the dishwasher."
- A popular manufactured fireplace log warns, "Caution— Risk of Fire."
- A box of birthday cake candles says, "DO NOT use soft wax as ear plugs or for any other function that involves insertion into a body cavity."
- A 13-inch wheel on a wheelbarrow warns, "Not intended for highway use."

CALL FORWARDING AT ——— BLANKETY-BLANK HOSPITAL

Darlene Sredl, PhD, RN

Thank you for calling Blankety-Blank Hospital. The following is a list of departments. Please indicate your preference by selecting the appropriate department numbers.

If you wish to speak to someone in the ED, dial "Edukashun."

If you wish to speak to someone in the OR, make up your mind first.

If you wish to speak to someone in ICU, make sure the video cable is connected to your head (set).

If you wish to speak to a proctologist, press number "2."

If you don't want to speak to a proctologist, press number "1" two times.

If at any time you are tempted to press "1," press "B4."

If you would like to speak to a dietician, press "8."

If this is an emergency, press "9."

If you are having an emergency that involves a proctologist, do *not* press 911!

Writer Wanted: Health Prevention

"Employment agency for health writers and editors has a client seeking an experienced associate-level editor with superb writing, reporting and editing skills. . . . The right candidate will be able to cover the latest advances in health prevention, diagnosis, treatment and research in a way that is technically sound, but with a personal tone."

—From a science writer's notice, August 2006. They didn't say whether the client sells tobacco, trans-fats, ethanol, or heroin.

TO AN AMŒBA

J. Lorch

Please dear cell, give us clue:
How we can become like you?
Always eating, never old,
Sexually completely cold.

Scientists, some influential,
Are impressed by your potential
Of eternal life on Earth.
You have neither death nor birth!
Gel to sol and sol to gel,
Life on Earth sure could be swell!

Some researchers old and dour
Say you're like a sack of flour,
Rolling down an inclined plane.
Surely they must be insane.

No one knows your secret code,
Except God—and Jacques Monod,
And perhaps Sir Francis Crick
With his beard so cute and chic.
Gel to sol and sol to gel,
They deserve the Prize Nobel.

Let us fix you on a slide,
Flattened out and frozen dried,
Brightly stained for all to see.
That's called cytochemistry.

See those granules purplish blue,
Varying in depth and hue?
Metachromasy for sure
(If, of course, the stain was pure).
Gel to sol and sol to gel,
Blue and purple suits you well.

Mitochondria? Maybe.
Golgi bodies? Possibly.
Artifacts? What blasphemy!
They are here for all to see.

Now we'll add some RNAse.
During the next interphase.
Blue spots are completely gone.
Enzymology is fun.
Gel to sol and sol to gel,
Brighten up your organelle.

The electron microscope
Gives us Vision, Faith, and Hope.
Structures hitherto unseen
Are unraveled in its beam.

Show your mucous coat's quite shabby
Like the fur of fighting tabby
And your membrane looks like hair
Of the Beatles, only fair.
Gel to sol and sol to gel,
Microscopes are made to sell.

Lysosome so like a dot,
Could be artifact—or not.
Fibrous protein here galore,
Microsomes and many more.

Keep your secret, keep it well.
Publications go to hell!
Let the others write a book.
I just like to sit and look:
Gel to sol and sol to gel
Pseudopods appear and swell.

If .mil became .nil, these would be choice domains:

zero.nil

nada.nil

nothing.nil

chocolateandvan.nil

PRODUCT WARNING LABELS

Susan Hewitt and Edward Subitzky

NEW GRAND UNIFIED THEORY DISCLAIMER:

The Manufacturer May Technically Be Entitled to Claim That
This Product Is Ten-Dimensional. However, the Consumer
Is Reminded That This Confers No Legal Rights Above
and Beyond Those Applicable to Three-Dimensional
Objects, Since the Seven New Dimensions Are Rolled Up
into Such a Small Area That They Cannot Be Detected.

PLEASE NOTE:

Some Quantum Physics Theories Suggest That
When the Consumer Is Not Directly Observing
This Product, It May Cease to Exist or Will Exist
Only in a Vague and Undetermined State.

HEALTH WARNING:

Care Should Be Taken When Lifting This Product
Because Its Mass, and Thus Its Weight, Depends
on Its Velocity Relative to the User.

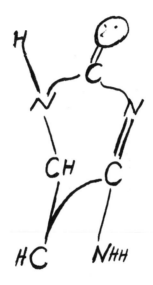

Cytosine

What did houseflies do before there were houses?

Notes to the Welfare Department

I am forwarding my marriage certificate and my
six children. I have seven but one died which
was baptized on a half sheet of paper.

I am writing to say that my baby was born
two years old, when do I get money?

Mrs. Jones has not had any clothing for a year
and has been visited regularly by the clergy.

I can get no sick pay, I have six children, can you tell me why?

I am glad to report that my husband who
was reported missing is now dead.

This is my 8th child, what are you going to do about it?

Please find for certain if my husband is dead. The man I live with now can't eat or do nothing until he knows for sure.

I am very much annoyed to find that you have branded my boy as illiterate, as this is a dirty lie. I was married to his father a week before he was born.

I am forwarding my marriage certificate and my three children one of which was a mistake as you will see.

In answer to your letter, I have given birth to a boy weighing ten pounds. I hope this is satisfactory.

My husband got his project cut off two weeks ago, and I haven't had any relief since.

Unless I get my husband's money soon, I
will be forced to lead an immoral life.

You have changed my little boy to a girl.
Will this make any difference.

Please send money at once as I have
fallen in error with my landlord.

I have no children as yet as my husband is a
bus driver and works day and night.

In accordance with instructions, I have given
birth to twins in the enclosed envelope.

I wants money as quick as I can get it. I have been in bed with
the doctor for two weeks and he doesn't do me no good. If
things don't improve, I will have to send for another doctor.

Di-hydroxy-chickenwire

114

Axioms

John F. Moffitt, PhD, Las Cruces, New Mexico

- I almost had a psychic girlfriend, but she left me before we met.
- Nobody ever listens to me; neither do I.
- How exactly do you determine when you're out of invisible ink?
- What's the speed of dark?
- What happens if you get scared half to death twice?
- It is axiomatic that axioms become clichés.

Celebrity Graphs

Lynne V. McFarland and Marc McFarland

BAR GRAPH: 007

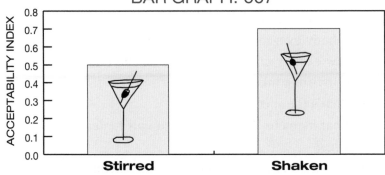

BUBBLE PLOT: LAWRENCE WELK

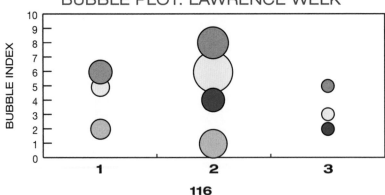

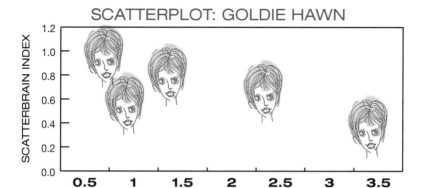

SCATTERPLOT: GOLDIE HAWN

SCATTERBRAIN INDEX

TIME (years)

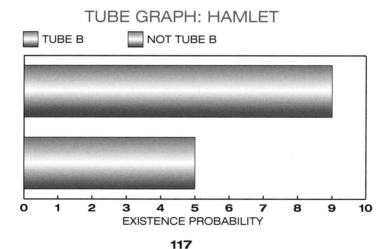

TUBE GRAPH: HAMLET

TUBE B   NOT TUBE B

EXISTENCE PROBABILITY

Scientists are saying
that the surface of the earth has
been getting brighter, but they're
not sure why. I can tell you one
thing: It's not the people.

—Comedian Shaun Eli Breidbart, www.BrainChampagne.com

The Beginning

X. Perry Mental

At a meeting with many speakers, there comes a moment when your name is called. A nice ploy to attract attention is to place yourself in the middle of the last row, so that when you are introduced, you raise half the row, step on their toes, proceed slowly to the front, and then start searching your pockets for a convoluted pack of lecture notes. Then you start searching for your reading glasses. If you find them, they are probably in an unexpected pocket. Next you proceed to read the paper, and we mean literally "read" it. This lecture technique is likened by Prof. Sabin to "kissing over a telephone: completely tasteless."

If you wish to put your audience to sleep as soon as possible, begin by enumerating all historically important papers published in the last fifty years that have any bearing on the subject. Another well-tested method is to start talking about something that has nothing to do with the subject by saying, for instance, "Before we turn to the discussion of . . ., let us shortly review. . . ."

Beginning at the beginning is an unpardonable mistake. Some speakers use the so-called multiple-colon technique. They say: "Mr. Chairman, I should like to say: the situation is as follows: I mean to say that: I should like to clarify in this lecture some points that are not sufficiently clear," and so on. If you continue for a few minutes in this vein, you lose the audience very soon.

A useful habit to distract the audience is to have a "tic," such as twitching one cheek, sniffling the nose, twisting the neck, or buttoning and unbuttoning your jacket. Putting on and removing reading glasses while you talk and glancing at the audience may sometimes replace such a tic. If you combine the tic with the glasses, all the stronger.

Some sophisticated speakers like to use quotations. Shakespeare, Einstein, and Wendell Holmes are quite safe. The trouble begins when the quotations are in the original Greek, Latin, Hebrew, or Sanskrit.

New Scientific Laws and Principles

- RULE OF ACCURACY: When you are working toward the solution of a problem, it always helps if you know the answer.

- RIDDLE'S CONSTANT: There are coexisting elements in frustrating phenomena that separate expected results from achieved results.

- HORNER'S FIVE-THUMB POSTULATE: Experience varies directly with equipment ruined.

- SKINNER'S CONSTANT (or Flannegan's Factor): The quantity that, when multiplied by, divided by, added to, or subtracted from the answer you get, gives you the answer you should have gotten.

- FIRST IRREPRODUCIBLE LAW: Publish first, confirm the experiment . . . later.

- It does not matter if you fall down as long as you pick up something from the floor while you get up. (Avery)

- Important advances are being made by young scientists who carry out experiments that old scientists said wouldn't work. (Westheimer)

- Problems worthy of attack prove their worth by hitting back. (Piet Hein)

- A successful symposium depends on the ratio of meeting to eating. (Zusmann)

Dipicolinic Acid

LAB PRODUCTIVITY CORRELATION TO SNACK SHOP VISITS

L. Boone, J. Collins, S. Winslow, C. Whitley, W. Rutala, D. Clanton, G. Stewart, J. Oakes, G. Peterman, D. Wennerstrom, S. Holcomb, S. Brown, J. Martin, and D. Roop, University of Tennessee

Single daily visits to the snack shop, both alone and in groups, enhance lab productivity. Daily visits greater than one correlate with decreases in lab productivity. As the number of participants in the visit increases, lab productivity falls drastically with each additional visit until it bottoms out at three Lab Productivity Index Units in the hole.

Lab Productivity Index:

9 = hours of active lab work on a day you thought was a site visit.

6 = hours in lab on a normal day, whether active or not.

3 = hours in lab on a day when the director or major professor was away.

0 = hours in lab on a day when the funding agency visits unexpectedly.

-3 = Hours/2 you said you were working in the lab last night.

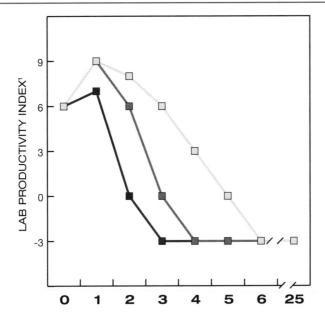

Figure 1A: Correlation between visits to the Snack Shop (SS) and Lab Productivity (LP). (—□—) alone; (—■—) groups of two; (—■—) groups larger than two.

This research was supported in part by Grant No. BLT-7UP-IOU-1.25. L.B. is a Snack Development Award recipient. S.W. is a UT Lunch Fellow. C.W. borrowed money from Ray. The authors wish to acknowledge Richard's Snack Shop for excellent technical assistance.

The Function of an Executive

Anonymous

As nearly everyone knows, an executive has practically nothing to do except to:

- Decide what is to be done.
- Tell somebody to do it.
- Listen to reasons why it should not be done, why it should be done by someone else, or why it should be done in a different way.
- Follow up to see whether the thing has been done.
- Discover it has not been done.
- Ask why it has not been done.
- Listen to excuses from the person who should have done it.
- Follow up again to see whether the thing has been done, only to discover it has been done incorrectly.
- Point out how it should have been done.
- Conclude that as long as it has been done it might as well be left where it is.

- Wonder whether it is time to get rid of a person who cannot do the thing right.
- Reflect that the person probably has a large family, and certainly any successor would be just as bad and may be worse.
- Consider how much simpler and better the thing would have been done if one had done it oneself in the first place.
- Reflect sadly that one could have done it right in twenty minutes, and now one has to spend two days to find out why it has taken three weeks for somebody else to do it wrong.

I had to buy a new can opener when the old one became a *can't* opener.

CLEAR AS A BELL———————————

E. E. Nikitin, "Optical Model for Spectator-Stripping Reactions," *Chemical Physics Letters,* 1967, 1, 266–268

Abstract: "An optical model for the harpooning reaction is discussed. It is suggested to use the widths of vibrational levels of a colliding molecule as an imaginary part of the complex potential describing elastic scattering and adsorption. Imaginary parts of phase shifts are calculated for a particular case."

P. Weiss, "Interaction Between Cells," *Reviews of Modern Physics,* 1959, 31, 454

"Clever getting around the acknowledgement of specificity in any one sector, whether by theoretical constructs or by unrealistic models, will not strip the other sectors of their aspects of specificity, and, hence, will not relieve the intellectual discomfort engendered by our inability to squeeze the broad subject of specificity into the limited conceptual framework which we have erected from the study of fragmentary vital phenomena lacking that aspect."

Metrologia Digitiales

H. S. Peiser

The Federated Cay States calls on scientists everywhere to substantiate the wisdom of their new system of measures, to expand that system consistent with its inherent and invariant philosophy, and to publish convincing reasons to be repeated by the public for abandoning the Système International (some pedants are forcing scientists into its use) and all attempts at metrication (a popular economic mirage for developing countries).

The Federated Cay States calls all countries to join in the simple Mono Treaty, laying down the compulsory use by all citizens of two (and only two) units of measure: the Mo and the No.

The Mo, or moment, is a measure of time interval.

The No, or numéro (French is so much more precise!), is the duodenary number.

All other units are illegal. All physical (and fiscal) phenomena must be monotonized (defined and measured in terms of Mos and Nos). In deference to history, SI prefixes are used, paired when convenient (mega-tera = 10^{16}).

The Mo is defined by the kMo, the interval between successive sunrises (allowance having been made for refractive index, relativistic, and other effects) on Pelican Cay at mean sea level on the day the inventor of the Mono System was born. The Mo is indistinguishable from the minute to a person without a chronometer, watch, or similar artificial device, and the kMo is closely similar to our old "day." These fortunate circumstances will make it so easy for the public to become monotonized.

TEN TENETS FOR TECHNICAL WRITING ——

Jack Eliezer

- Use words that mean only what you want them to mean, and don't let on to the perplexed reader. (One professor actually wrote to me, "The earth has no boundaries, yet it is finite!")

- Always expound in pompous polysyllables employing current buzzwords and expostulating with circumlocutory verbosity.

- Synthesize ingenious concatenations of sonorous phrases with negligible congruity.

- Use surreptitious recourse to arcane etymology to inculcate an impression of coruscating erudition.

- Compound your syntax with ambivalent and equivocal periphrasis to attain esoteric obfuscation.

- Resort to immutable quantifications to purvey an aura of punctilious erudition.

- Sporadically resuscitate your reader from somnolent stupor by bombastic superlatives and fustian imperatives.

- Intersperse your thematic opus with technological nomenclature without terminological redundancies to promote extirpating turbidity and deleterious opacity.

- Preclude untenable allegations which can be repudiated by fractious readers incensed enough to do so, with opprobrious effects to yourself.

- Never write as one speaks.

OUR GUARANTEE OF
BUG-FREE PROGRAMS

David W. Deley, members.cox.net/deleyd/

OUR LIMITED TIME GUARANTEE

All programs and utilities are hereby guaranteed to be free from defects in workmanship and programming for a period of one minute after initial release. After that, you must refer below to the fully limited lifetime warranty. This guarantee does not cover damage due to accident, misuse, abuse, negligence, or incompetence. We are not responsible for any incidental or consequential damage that might occur as a result of the explicit or implicit use of these programs, including the possible complete destruction of all software on said machine, including said machine itself, along with the building containing said machine, and various parts of the surrounding countryside. This guarantee is valid only in the United States, except for southern California, and only between the hours of 8:00 A.M. and 5:00 P.M. whenever we feel like it. Void where prohibited.

OUR FULLY LIMITED LIFETIME WARRANTY
In the event one of our utilities does not function properly due to faulty workmanship or programming logic:

- For a period of one month after initial release, we will listen to your complaints and smile politely, occasionally nodding the head as if in agreement.
- For a period of one year after initial release, we will supply, at no charge to the user, sympathy and commiseration over any component of a program found to be inadequate.

This warranty gives you specific rights, and you may have other rights that vary from state to state; that is, the state (of mind) you are in may affect the intensity of our sympathy.

THE SEASIDE LABORATORY FLOATS
A PROPOSAL, FROM SINKINGS, 3(1)

Submitted by Samuel P. Meyers

DR. KAISER EMIGLIANO has received $867,483.73 from the National Science Foundation for a one-year feasibility study to transversely saw Virginia Key from its base and float it. This project will provide valuable clues to the Pleistocene geology of our tight little isostatic island and yield valuable fossils to be sold at the Seaquarium to replenish the long-suffering overhead account.

The remarkable concept is for the "visiting institution" to replace the "visiting scientist." This breakthrough will enable our entire institute to be towed to other areas for six to twelve months, depending on tidal flow and neglecting geostrophic forces. This will eliminate the need for sabbatical leaves and vacation periods. Mr. Truly Illman reports that this also will greatly reduce paperwork for travel forms because only a single form will be needed. Instead of individual scientists attending meetings, the entire institute could be represented! The prestige value alone is staggering. Site visitations by National Science Foundation committees could be eliminated because the institute could visit the committee wherever it is. The proposed move would eventually eliminate the need for research grants because floating institutions would be considered research vessels and thus eligible for block funding.

Woods Hole Oceanographic Institution is cross-cutting their peninsula in a gallant but dastardly attempt to be the first all-afloat institute. Scripps Institution of Oceanography poses a definite threat to our progress because they are located (at the time of this writing) on the San Andreas fault and need perhaps only a slight push to become insular.

The Seaside Laboratory
University of Southernmost Florida
1.25 Ricketyback Causeway
Miami, Florida 33169

Li$^+$ ion

SEMINAL IDEA OF THE MONTH CLUB (SIOTMC)

Graduate students and scholars can receive assistance in meeting publication requirements, preparing seminar papers, and so on. SIOTMC provides you with research ideas, capable (with further work) of yielding publishable papers and monographs.

Seminal ideas are available in the following sections, one of which each member enrolls in:

- Humanities

- Social sciences

- Physical sciences and mathematics

- Biological sciences

- Sections in earth science and engineering are planned for the future.

Each member agrees to accept three seminal ideas a year (at an average price of $4 to $12.50 per idea), except during sabbaticals, when only one need be accepted. In addition, the purchase of three seminal ideas entitles you to one bonus idea free. No seminal idea is offered to more than one scholar at a time. Both synthetic and analytic ideas are available.

For further information and details, with no obligation, write to Seminal Idea of the Month Club.

POPULAR LAWS OF PHYSICS WHERE **LOVE** REPLACES LIGHT OR MATTER

Jason Bennett and Sadie Dingfelder

♥ It may seem strange to you that love can function as both a particle and wave, but this is the nature of love.

♥ An astronaut who leaves Earth in a spaceship that travels near the speed of love will return to Earth younger than his twin brother.

♥ There is a tiny, nonzero possibility that the love you see here on Earth could in the next moment exist in the Andromeda galaxy.

♥ If there are higher dimensions of love, they are tightly wrapped in tiny balls we cannot perceive.

The Turbo-Encabulator

Bernard Salwen

For a number of years, work has been proceeding to bring perfection to the crudely conceived idea of a machine that would not only supply inverse reactive current for use in unilateral phase detractors but would also be capable of automatically synchronizing cardinal grammeters. Such a machine is the Turbo-Encabulator.

Basically, the only new principle involved is that instead of power being generated by the relative motion of conductors and fluxes, it is produced by the medial interaction of magneto-reluctance and capacitive directance.

The original machine had a base plate of prefabulated amulite, surmounted by a malleable logarithmic casing.

That way, the two spurving bearings were in direct line with the penta-metric fan. The latter consisted simply of six hydro-coptic marzel vanes, so fitted to the ambi-facient lunar wane-shaft that side fumbling was effectively prevented. The main winding was of the normal lotus-0-delta type, placed in pan-endermic semi-boloid slots in the stator, every seventh conductor being connected by a non-reversible tremie pipe to the differential gridle-spring on the "up" end of the grammeters.

Forty-one manestically spaced grouting brushes were arranged to feed into the rotor slipstream a mixture of high–S-value phenyl-hydro-benzamine and 5% remanative tetryl-iodo-hexamine.

Both of these liquids have specific pericosities given by $P = 2.5Cn^{6.7}$, where n is the diathetical evolute of retrograde temperature phase disposition, and C is Cholmondeley's annular grillage coefficient.

Initially, n was measured with the aid of a metapolar refractive pil-frometer, but up to the present nothing has been found to equal the transcendental hopper dadoscope.

Electrical engineers will appreciate the difficulty of nubing together a regurgitative pur-well and a supramitive wennel-sprock. Indeed, this proved to be a stumbling block until it was found that the use of anhydrous nangling pins enabled a krypto-nastic boiling shim to be tankered.

The early attempts to construct a sufficiently robust spiral decommutator failed, largely because of a lack of appreciation of the large quasipiestic stresses in the gremlin studs.

The latter were specially designed to hold the roffit bars to the spam-shaft.

However, when it was discovered that wending could be prevented by a simple addition to the living sockets, almost perfect running was secured.

The operating point is maintained as near as possible to the H.F. rem peak by constantly fromaging the bitumogenous spandrels.

This is a distinct advance on the standard nivel-sheave.

No dramcock oil is required after the phase detractors have been remissed.

Undoubtedly, the turbo-encabulator has now reached a very high level of technical development.

It has been successfully used for operating nofer trunnions. In addition, whenever a bar-escent skor motion is required, it may be employed in conjunction with a drawn reciprocating dingle arm to reduce sinusoidal depleneration.

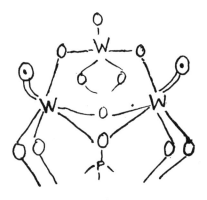

Phosphotungstate radical

A VERBAL RORSCHACH:
AN ANTIDOTE FOR TECHNICALLY OBNUBILATED APPELLATION

E. J. Helwig

WORDS, LIKE THE RORSCHACH ink blots, carry some sort of impression. Scholarly articles must sound scientific, esoteric, and prestigious. Because the recondite is often confused with the erudite, titles of technical articles often smother meaning under a plethora of jargon.

The following titles were gleaned from a list of technical papers. A possible Rorschach interpretation follows each.

- Representative Mixing in U12. Social Life on an Atomic Submarine.

- Double Image Formation in a Stratified Medium. Visual Aberration in a Stoned Spiritualist.

- Wave Motion Due to Impulsive Twist on the Surface. Math à Go-Go, in the Surf.

- Fluid Behavior in Parabolic Containers Undergoing Vertical Excitation. Standing Room Only at the Burlesque.

- Many Body Theory. Life in a Harem.

- Some Results of Transport Theory and Their Application of Monte Carlo Methods. Hitchhiking Home from Las Vegas.

- Dispersion Techniques in Field Theory. Fun on a Field Trip.

- Wullenweber Arrays Using Doublet Aerials. A Death-Defying Double Trapeze Act Featuring the Famous Flying Wullenwebers.

Now that you know how verbal Rorschach testing works, go to your own technical publications and try it with some friends.

Saga of a New Hormone

Norman Applezweig

I n recent months we've learned of the discovery of three miracle drugs by three leading pharmaceutical houses. On closer inspection it appears that all three products are one and the same hormone. If you're at all curious about how more than one name can apply to the same compound, it might be worth examining the chain of events that occurs in the making of a miracle drug.

The physiologist usually discovers it first, quite accidentally, while looking for two other hormones. He gives it a name intended to denote its function in the body, and predicts that the new compound should be useful in treating a rare blood disease. From one ton of beef glands, fresh from the slaughterhouse, he finally isolates 10 grams of the pure hormone, which he turns over to the physical chemist for characterization.

The physical chemist finds that 95% of the physiologist's purified hormone is an impurity, and that the remaining 5% contains at least three different compounds. From one of these

149

he successfully isolates 10 milligrams of the pure crystalline hormone. On the basis of its physical properties, he predicts possible structure, and suggests that the function of the new compound is probably different from that assigned to it by the physiologist. He changes its name and turns it over to the organic chemist for confirmation of structure.

The organic chemist does not confirm the structure suggested by the physical chemist. Instead, he finds that it differs by only one methyl group from a new compound recently isolated from watermelon rinds, which, however, is inactive. He gives it a chemical name, accurate but too long and unwieldy for common use. The compound is therefore named after the organic chemist for brevity. He finally synthesizes 10 grams of the hormone, but tells the physiologist he's sorry that he can't spare even a gram because it is all needed for the preparation of derivatives and further structural studies. He gives him instead 10 grams of the compound isolated from watermelon rinds.

The biochemist suddenly announces that he has discovered the new hormone in the urine of pregnant sows. Because it is easily split by the crystalline enzyme he has isolated from the salivary glands of the South American earthworm, he insists that the new compound is obviously the cofactor for vitamin

B_{16}, whose lack accounts for the incompleteness of the pyruvic acid cycle in annelids. He changes its name.

The physiologist writes to the biochemist requesting a sample of his earthworms.

The nutritionist finds that the activity of the new compound is identical with factor PFF, which he has recently isolated from chick manure and which is essential to the production of pigment in fur-bearing animals. Because both PFF and the new hormone contain the trace element zinc, fortification of white bread with the substance will lengthen the lifespan and stature of future generations, he assures us. To indicate the compound's nutritive importance, he changes its name.

The physiologist writes the nutritionist for a sample of PFF. Instead he receives 1 pound of the raw material from which it is obtained.

The pharmacologist decides to study the effect of the compound on gray-haired rats. He finds to his dismay that they lose their hair after one injection. Because this does not happen in castrated rats, he decides that the drug works synergistically with the sex hormone testosterone, and therefore antagonizes the gonadotropic factor of the pituitary. Observing that the new compound is an excellent vasoconstrictor, the pharmacologist concludes that it should make a good nose-drop preparation. He changes its name and sends twelve bottles of nose drops, together with a spray applicator, to the physiologist.

The clinician receives samples of the pharmacologist's product for testing in patients who have head colds. He finds it only mildly effective in relief of nasal congestion, but is amazed to discover that three of his head cold sufferers who are also the victims of a rare blood disease have suddenly been dramatically cured.

He gets the Nobel Prize.

"WHAT BURNS ME UP IS THAT HE'S HERE ON A GRANT TO STUDY BIRTH CONTROL."

CONFERENCEMANSHIP: INSTRUCTIONS FOR PRESENTING SCIENTIFIC PAPERS

Professor Jahn N. Droughzee, Chairman of the Bored, SPCL

(Society for the Production of Cruelty to Listeners)

IN PRESENTING A TEN-MINUTE paper, remember that the audience has more interest in fishing or baseball than in what you may say. Try not to rile them. While speaking, face the board or screen, but do not face the audience; someone might recognize you. Speak low, and slur your words. This will quiet jaded nerves. Don't raise your voice to emphasize a point—you might wake someone. A purring pitch, like a distant waterfall, is soothing and soporific.

Plan your speech to be half finished when the chairman flashes the nine-minute signal. Don't tell the audience what you are going to talk about. Let them guess. Plunge right into details. There is nothing as unscientific as incomplete evidence. Assume they are novices in your field and want to know everything. Therefore, use symbols and abbreviations, and coin new words if necessary. They save space and breath. Don't use standard terminology. Latin names are always good, usually as good as BNA, DNA, RNS, OPA, and PUA.

Put every scrap of experimental data on your tables and graphs. Don't suppress vital information—after all, this is science, not journalism. Insert all pertinent and impervious data, so as to cover most of the slide. Lettering should be microscopic so you can get more on. It should take at least five minutes to read each slide, but show it only for thirty seconds.

Don't label curves or coordinates, and never summarize or draw conclusions. Someone might challenge you in the discussion period. Finish by reading several columns of numbers. If you must draw a conclusion, do so after the gong rings, and then leave.

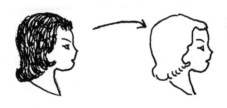

Oxidation

Zilch Gas

Sydney Abbey, Institute for the
Disproof of Intellectually Offensive Theories

"Zilch gas" is a generic name for numerous malodorous volatile substances. The name was intended to honor the life work of the late No Bull Prize winner Elmer P. Zilch.

Zilch gas was to be achieved by reacting zinc with iodine in the presence of hydrochloric acid:

$$2Zn + I_2 + HCl \rightarrow 2Zilch + N_2$$

Every attempt to prepare Zilch resulted in a violent explosion. The cause was thought to be the production of hydrogen by the side reaction between the acid and the zinc. That is, insufficient iodine was present.

PAPER CHORMATOGRAPHY

Ralph A. Lewin, Scripps Institution of Oceanography

In these days of neoclassical renaissance, when it seems that everybody above the rank of laboratory assistant is "charismatic" and every institution beyond the junior college level is "prestigious," we should not fail to note the grwoth of what may be called "paper chormatography" (from the mythical Greek *chorma*, gen. *chormatos*, "an inversion," and *graphein*, "to write").

With the further limitation of research grants and the general need for scientists to type their laboratory reprots themselves, chormatographic phenomena will undoubtedly become more and more evident as time goes on.

I first because aware of the phenomenon when I was typing the penultimate draft of my thesis on the genetics of *Chalmydomonas*. I wasted a lot of time, carefully retyping the word *Chalmydomonas*, before before I realized what was going on, and capitulated to what is clearly a force of nature. I am sure that all biochemists who have used slat gradients to elute unknown substances from columns will know what I mean. My brother-in-law Gerlad, a mathematician, has had the same trouble with calaculus.

We are planning a symposium on the grwoth of chormatography. Those wishing to participate should contact the author.

Wanted

ON ANY TERMS

A REWARD IS OFFERED FOR
INFORMATION LEADING TO THE ARREST OF

EDDY CURRENT

charged with the induction of an eighteen-year-old coil, called Milli Henry, found half choked, and with the theft of valuable joules. This unrectified criminal, armed with carbon rod, escaped from Weston Primary Cell, where he had been clapped in ions. The escape was planned in three phases. First, he fused the electrolytes, then he climbed through a grid despite the impedance of warders, and finally he ran to earth in a nearby magnetic field. He has been missing since Faraday. Watt seems most likely is that he stole an AC motor. This is of low capacity, and he is expected to change it for a megacycle, and return ohm by a short circuit. He may offer series resistance and is a potential killer.

FROM R. M. KLEIN AND G. K. K. LINK,
"THE ETIOLOGY OF CROWN GALL,"
QUARTERLY REVIEW OF BIOLOGY, 1955,
30, 207

> "A change elicited by an affect or effect or by an affectant in
> the affectee is a passive or active response affect or response
> effect. If it counters the affect or effect or the affectant which
> elicits it, it is an active counter-affect or counter-effect. If it is
> an active counter affect or effect, it is a counter active affect or
> effect, i.e., a reaction in the strict sense of the term as used by
> pathologists."

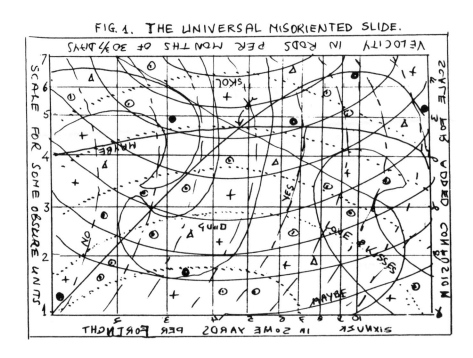

FIG. 1. THE UNIVERSAL MISORIENTED SLIDE.

162

MORE MATHEMATICAL TERMS FOR SOCIAL DESCRIPTION

Henry Winthrop, University of South Florida

- **Invariant:** A behavior of a chairman, director, etc., that remains the same under all administrative transformations, as in the French maxim that the more things change, the more they stay the same.

- **Irrational expression:** Any comment at variance with the views of the prevailing clique in any department.

- **Klein bottle:** Any faculty member lacking both inner resources and external front, who is completely one-sided in point of view.

- **Lattice structure:** A situation that looks equally fouled up in all directions from whatever angle it is viewed.

- **Least squares:** The salvageable remnant among academic organization members.

From the *Annual Report* of Botanical Gardens Department, Singapore, 1961

"Long tailed macaque monkeys (*Macaca irus*) plague the lives of the staff of the Botanic Gardens in Singapore. Last year none were caught in traps and only 4 were shot. Shooting is regarded as being of little avail, however, as a single shot will scatter all the monkeys tree-top wise to safety, then they pour vituperation on the helpless garden's staff. The fact that the office shotgun was found to have bent barrels did little to improve matters."

Synthetic Happiness

G. van den Bergh, Haarlem, the Netherlands*

After many years of research, a team of scientific workers under Professor Sadler of Amsterdam University has succeeded in producing synthetic happiness. Although the quantity is still negligible, there have already been some successful experiments on people, and the mass production of synthetic happiness is only a matter of time (1).

The research team took as a starting point the common experience that happiness is not where you look for it. Instead of giving up, they redoubled their efforts, with success.

The first thought of Professor Sadler proved to be useless. If simply all feelings, thoughts, experiences, and situations were to be studied, the problem could be solved. But it soon appeared that even the best computer would need 3.1×10^{11} years to complete the task, provided that the number of possible combinations remained constant. Because the number of possibilities increases every year by about 10 million, the method did not seem very promising.

Eventually the scientists succeeded in constructing a simple electronic brain, which seeks where it does not seek. Thus happiness could easily be located and isolated. It proved to be very volatile, and extremely difficult to analyze chemically.

Another problem was how to produce happiness in usable form. Experience has shown that an uncontrolled explosion of happiness has effects similar to those of other explosives, including the atom bomb. Blindness and deafness are the most common effects. In more serious cases, the brain is blown out, and a serious disorder of the heart ensues.

The scientists have happiness under control and may produce any amount of it in a reasonable time. However, before the economic exploitation of happiness can begin, there is still another problem to solve, because happiness cannot be bought. It has not yet been possible to sell any amount of happiness without rapid denaturation of it.

There are different approaches to the problem of selling happiness. Some lawyers assert that there is no problem in constructing a form of buying and selling that is not buying and selling. Professor Sadler seeks a transaction-resistant happiness by a chemical method. His sponsor, General Happiness Inc., has granted another $1.5 million for this research.

There seem to be serious political implications for the exploitation of happiness. Political observers state the possibility of a social revolution, after which everybody would have as much happiness as he or she liked. Some political parties have already urged their governments to prevent this.

So for a while we shall still have to do with ordinary happiness.

*It is reported that the author has found nonsynthetic happiness.
1. Aldous Huxley, *Brave New World*, 1947.

THOUGHTS AFTER HEARING ⸺
A. A. MILNE READ TO A CHILD

J. R. Christensen

I think I'll be a scientist, exploring the unknown.
I've always wished to be one, at least since I've been grown.
I'll be a grave astronomer, agazing out past Mars
At silent, spinning nebulæ; at darkly shining stars.
Or be an anthropologist—"The proper study: man."
I'm feeling rather funny, and I don't know what I am.
So 'round and 'round about and 'round about I go,
'Round about the quandary, the quandary of the cosmos.

I'll be a new-biologist, and think about the gene.
Or maybe a virologist; keep watch on the unseen.
I could be a geologist; find faults and study strata.
Or a stolid statistician; make the most of meager data.
I think I'll be a chemist; deal with molecules complex–
A specialist in DNA, with abstract views on sex.
Perhaps I'll solve a problem, which will help to solve a
    problem,
Which will help to solve a problem, which really isn't there.

Psychology attracts me: mind seeking to know mind.
As a medical researcher, could I hope to help mankind?
Perhaps I'll be a physicist, with mesons, pi and mu.
Or be a biochemist, and measure Q O_2.
Or deal with pure mathematics, thus establish QED.
Oh! I'm feeling quite peculiar, and I don't know what to be!
So 'round about and 'round about and '*round* about and
    'Round about and '*Round* about and 'ROUND about I go.

Twitter-ion

Rudin's Law:
When two or more pairs of numbers occur together, rank order and correlate.

FROM D. CAUSEY, "CRIMES IN SCIENTIFIC EDITING," *TURTOX NEWS*, 1959, 37(3), 93

"Editors are, in my opinion, a low form of life, inferior to the viruses and only slightly above academic deans."

PSYCHIATRIC TREATMENT OF ———
UNBALANCED MAMMALIAN CELLS

R. G. Veal, University of Rocky Mountains, Estes Park, Colorado

The effect of reversible killing of mammalian cells by unbalancing was demonstrated by De Mars; he used euploid, N-16-fed, primary hamster ovary cells.

In our experiment the cells were obtained from chopped ovaries. After trypsinization and centrifugation, the cell sediment was very carefully unbalanced on an analytical balance.

The unbalanced cells were then resuspended in a nutrient medium containing fluctuating concentrations of essential salts, amino acids, vitamins, and iron. The presence of iron permitted achievement of additional unbalance by the use of a magnetic stirrer.

Following the treatment, the unbalanced cells were psychoanalyzed by one of the methods advocated by Freud.[1]

The results of this experiment are yet inconclusive; their statistical significance is not being evaluated.

---

1. S. Freud, "Application of Analytical Methods to Early Trauma in Fœtal Cells," *J. Cytol. Psychol.,* 1899, 88, 12–17.

CONFERENCEMANSHIP:
NOISE DENSITY OF CONFERENCES

Alexander Kohn

CONFERENCES AND SYMPOSIA ARE far apart, and it has become fashionable to arrange them in small and hidden resorts. In addition to guests who have to pay their own expenses, a limited number of speakers are well taken care of by the organizers. These speakers, more often than not, have to travel great distances. It has now become a custom to invite a lecture limited to a certain number of words (the excuse being time limitation) and to pay according to that length. This means the speaker is paid so many dollars per so many miles traveled. Hence there is a correlation between the number of words and the number of miles traveled.

Thus, Personal Conference Importance Value (PCIV) may be expressed as

$$PCIV \sim Miles/Words$$

It is obvious that a speaker in a local affair where he drones on for an hour or two, having traveled only 15 miles, cannot compete with a scientist who flies from Jerusalem to Rio de Janeiro to deliver a talk of only 1,000 words.

However, this value is not the sole index of the importance of a speaker. One must also take into account the number of people who come to listen, and from how far. The modified PCIV is proportional to

Miles/People

The number of people is put in the denominator, because as things are nowadays, the more important you are, the more select is your audience, and not everybody may come.

Combining the two fractions, one arrives at a formula:

$$PCIV = (Miles/Words) \times (Miles/People)$$
$$= Square\ Miles/(Words \times People)$$

The last expression is obviously a reciprocal of noise density, that is, a function of number of words emitted by a number of people per unit of area.

Who is surprised by this correlation between importance of a speaker and the reciprocal of noise density?

There was a nice model of DNA fame

Who helically played the genetical game

A sort of a trick

Of Watson and Crick

That promoted our knowledge as
    well as their name.

BASIC SCIENCE

Basic science
Has to do with isotopes and ions
Sols and gels
Inorganic and organic smells
And variously differentiated cells
In this scientific mélange.

Plus *c'est la même chose, plus ça change*
What people write
Was out of date on the previous night
No sooner do you see data neatly analyzed
Than BOOM comes another research
And the facts are changed.

To call this "basic" is exaggeration
Science is too ephemeral, too full of imitation
A foundation or basis
Should have homeostasis
That which is basic is Art
Of which Science is a metaplastic part.

DEFINITIONS CONTRIBUTED BY DR. KABAT

Reputation (bad): He is not always wrong. He is not that reliable.

Scientific career can be divided into three periods. In the first, the scientist works. In the second, he talks about the work. In the third, he says, "Let me show you my Institute."

PECULIAR RELATIONSHIPS BETWEEN AUTHORS AND THE SUBJECTS OF THEIR STUDIES

Alexander Kohn

It has often amazed us how the choice of subject of a study seems to relate to the author's name.

Recently Lord Brain reviewed brain mechanism and models (1); together with Head, he has his ideas about *The Man and His Ideas* (2). Some Foxes dealt with rats and dogs: One Fox (3) studies the effect of trypan blue on rat embryos, and another Fox psychoanalyzed dogs (4). Harm (5) showed that trypan blue was harmful to rabbit embryos. Born et al. (6) measured the changes in the heart and lungs at birth. It is a little strange that Bacon (7) studied sugars in the blood of sheep. Quite understandably, Amoroso (8) was interested in endocrinology of pregnancy and Seegal in immunofertility (9).

For people interested in tissue cultures and religion, we recommend the paper by Pious and Hamburger (10), who studied fifty cultures of human foreskin cells. Data of Price (11) were used to compute values. For botanists we suggest Pond's paper on aquatic plants (12), and for those interested in female anatomy we suggest the paper of Goodheart on toplessness (13).

Our attention was also attracted to some books: Dull and Dull wrote a book on mathematics for engineers (14), and Glasscock is the author of isotopic gas analysis for biochemists (15). Biology of the laboratory mouse was written by C. C. Little (16), while Smaller dealt with the structure of biomolecules (which are smaller still) (17). It is surely coincidence that Hand wrote about the management of bilateral undescended testes (18) and that Professor Fleisch wrote a book on proper nutrition (19).

1. Lord Brain, "Brain Mechanisms and Models," *Nature,* 1964, 203, 3.

2. Brain, R., and Head, H., "The Man and His Ideas," *Brain,* 1961, 84, 561.

3. Fox, H. M., et al., "Effect of Trypan Blue on Rat Embryo," *Proc. Amer. Assoc. Anatomists,* Buffalo, 1958.

4. Fox, H. W., "A Sociosexual Behaviour Abnormality in the Dog Resembling Oedipus Complex in Man," *J. Am. Vet. Med. Assoc.,* 1964, 144, 868.

5. Harm, H., "Der Einfluss von Trypanblau auf die Nachkommenschaft traechtiger Kaninchen," *Z. Naturforsch.,* 1964, 9b, 536.

6. Born, G. V. R., et al., "Changes in the Heart and Lungs at Birth," *Cold Spring Harbor Symposium,* 1954, 19, 102.

7. Bacon, J. S. D., "Fructose and Glucose in Blood of Fetal Sheep," *Biochem. J.,* 1948, 42, 397.

8. Amoroso, E. C., "Third Intl. Rheumatology Congress," *Brit. Med. J.,* 1955, ii, 117.

9. Seegal, B. C., *Symp. in Immunofertility,* La Jolla, Calif., Population Council, 1962, 215.

10. Pious D. A., Hamburger R. N., and Miles, S. E., "Clonal Growth of Primary Human Cell Cultures," *Exp. Cell. Research,* 1964, 33, 495.

11. Price, W. C., "Thermal Inactivation Rates of Four Plant Viruses," *Arch. Ges. Virusforsch.,* 1940, 1, 373.

12. Pond, R. H., "The Biological Relation of Aquatic Plants to the Substratum," *US Fish Commission,* 1901, 483–525.

13. Goodheart, C. B., "A Biological View of Toplessness," *New Scientist,* Sep. 3, 1964, 558.

14. Dull, R. N., and Dull, R., *Mathematics for Engineers,* 3d ed., McGraw Hill, 1951.

15. Glasscock, R., *Isotopic Gas Analysis for Biochemists,* Academic Press, 1954.

16. Little, C. C., *Biology of the Laboratory Mouse,* Dover, 1956.

17. Smaller, B. *Structure of Biomolecules,* ed. Duchesne, Wiley, 1963.

18. Hand, J. R., "Management of Bilateral Undescended Testes," *Postgrad. Med.,* 1963, 33, 480.

19. Fleisch, A., *Ernaehren wir uns richtig,* Thieme Verlag, 1961.

$$H_2O = HIJKLMNO$$

PRODUCT WARNING LABELS

Susan Hewitt and Edward Subitzky

ADVISORY:

There Is an Extremely Small but Nonzero Chance
That, Through a Process Known as Tunneling, This
Product May Spontaneously Disappear from Its
Present Location and Reappear at Any Random Place
in the Universe, Including Your Neighbor's Domicile.
The Manufacturer Will Not Be Responsible for Any
Damages or Inconvenience That May Result.

READ THIS BEFORE OPENING PACKAGE:

According to Certain Suggested Versions of the
Grand Unified Theory, the Primary Particles
Constituting This Product May Decay to
Nothingness Within the Next 400 Million Years.

THIS IS A 100% MATTER PRODUCT:

In the Unlikely Event That This Merchandise
Contacts Antimatter in Any Form, a
Catastrophic Explosion Will Result.

185

Don't anthropomorphize computers. They hate it!

—Spotted on Slashdot.com

CURIOUS CHOICES OF COLLABORATORS

Alexander Kohn

The belletristical value of a scientific publication is much enhanced by a proper choice of collaborating author. Notable combinations include Ham and Plate (1); I. M. Tough, Brown Court, and King (2); German and Bird (3); Grey, Mutton, et al. (4); Holland and Doll (5); and Chu and You (6). The most famous in physics is Alpher, Bethe, and Gamow: αβγ (7).

When the authors prefer to stay single, they may have good reasons for doing so. It would be embarrassing for Poor (8) and Fortune (9) to appear together. The collaboration of Sell (10) and Favour (11) would not make a favorable impression. More convincing might be the co-authorship of Noyes (12), Ohno (13), and Ghosh (14), or of Main (15) and Journey (16).

1. Ham, J. S., and Plate, J. R., *J. Chem. Phys.,* 1952, 20, 335.

2. Tough, I. M., Brown Court, and King, M. J., *Lancet,* 1962, ii, 335.

3. German, J. L., and Bird, C. E., *Lancet,* 1961, ii, 48.

4. Grey, J. E., Mutton, D. E., and Ashby, A. V., *Lancet,* 1962, i, 21.

5. Holland, W. W., and Doll, R., *Br. J. Cancer,* 1962, 16, 177.

6. Chu, J. P., and You, S. S., *J. Endocrinol.,* 1946, 4, 392.

7. Alpher, R. A., Bethe, H., and Gamow, G., "The Origin of Chemical Elements," *Physical Review,* 1948, 73, 803.

8. Poor, E., *Transplantation Bull.,* 1957, 4, 143.

9. Fortune, D. W., *Lancet,* 1962, i, 537.

10. Sell, K. W., et al., "Research in Burns," *Am. Inst. Biol. Sci.,* 1962, 351.

11. Favour, C. B., *Ann. N.Y. Acad. Sci.,* 1958, 73, 590.

12. Noyes, W. V., *Virology,* 1962, 17, 282.

13. Ohno, S., *Lancet,* 1962, ii, 152.

14. Ghosh, D. K., and Whiffen, D. H., *Mol. Phys.,* 1959, 2, 285.

15. Main, B., *J. Natl. Cancer Inst.,* 1955, 15, 1023.

16. Journey, L. J., et al., *Cancer Res.,* 1962, 22, 998.

Axioms

John F. Moffitt, PhD, Las Cruces, New Mexico

- Modern art presents hope that, perhaps, things may not be quite as bad as they are now painted.
- Real equality exists: A female blockhead is as likely now to become a boss as is a male cretin.
- Half the people are below average.
- When everything is coming your way, you're in the wrong lane.
- Youth is a blunder, maturity a struggle, old age but idle regrets.
- Aging goes on for a very long time—but only if you're lucky.
- Longer life means less future to worry about.
- A clear conscience is usually the sign of a bad memory.
- Experience teaches us that no one ever learns from experience.

Gold-Plated Chain

Improvement and Deletion of Memory

L. Forgetful

Animals subjected to electric shocks a short time after learning to run a maze forget what they learned.

It is not sufficient just to give the animals electric shocks. They have to be applied across the animals' heads (1). Shocking the feet will not obliterate memory. Applying the shock across the head four hours after the animal has learned a task has no effect on retaining the new ability.

On the other hand, treatment with strychnine improves learning and the consolidation of the memory (2).

Strychnine was therefore administered daily at sublethal dose to half of a class of human volunteers,* the other half of the class serving as controls. In the survivors of the test group, a statistically significant improvement in problem solving capacity was evident, provided that the strychnine was given about 30 minutes before beginning the lesson.

Although, according to Cameron (3), oral administration of RNA increased memory retention in the aged, it was not used in our studies because of its side effects such as lowering blood pressure and causing pains in the gastrointestinal tract.

1. Thompson, C. W., *Can. J. Psychol.,* 1961, 15, 67.

2. McGaugh, J. L., and Petrinovitch, L., *Am. J. Psychol.,* 1959, 72, 99.

3. Cameron, E., *New York Times,* May 7, 1962, 34.

*Subnormal children aged two to four, from an orphanage (cf. Schwarz, A., et al., *JAMA,* 1960, 173, 861).

Wacky Warning Labels

Robert B. Dorigo Jones,
Michigan Lawsuit Abuse Watch, www.mlaw.org

- A massage chair warns, "Do not use massage chair without clothing. . . . Never force any body part into the backrest area while the rollers are moving."
- A cardboard car sunshield to keep sunlight off the dashboard warns, "Do not drive with sunshield in place."
- An "Aim-n-Flame" fireplace lighter cautions, "Do not use near fire, flame or sparks."
- A label on a hand-held massager advises consumers not to use "while sleeping or unconscious."
- A 12-inch rack for storing compact disks warns, "Do not use as a ladder."
- A laser printer cartridge warns, "Do not eat toner."

Alanine

What Do You Call All Those Physicians?

Seth L. Haber, Kaiser Foundation Hospitals

*C*ollectively, they are a bore; in conventions, frequently a caution. Medical students often are a disappointment, interns a trial or a tribulation. Residents come by the rotunda, although I have heard some refer to a term of residents.

Orthopedists are a brace, osteopaths a joint, and podiatrists a parade. Dermatologists are a rash. Surgeons are an incision, a pack, or a stitch. Many an anesthesiologist is a gasser. Neurologists are a twitch or a bundle. Analysts are a dream, virologists a strain, psychologists a complex, immunologists a complement, and gastroenterologists a rumble or an eructation. Cardiologists are a thrill, flutter, or murmur; diagnosticians a guess; hematologists a clump or a blast; and radiologists a ray or a screen.

Of course, gynecologists are a sexion or a smear, cytologists are a cell, obstetricians are a labor or a nursery, and pediatricians are a squall. Urologists must be a stream or a puddle. Proctologists are a pile or a reaming. Otolaryngologists are a gaggle, otologists are a herd, and ophthalmologists an ogle. Anatomists are a corps. Pathologists are a section or a tissue—some say a lesion. Occasionally, hospital administrators may be a plague.

Irreproducibility in Mammals

Mortimer Lorber, MD, Georgetown University

The breeding of a male donkey with a female horse reproducibly causes an irreproducible result. Based on the major characteristics of the offspring, I have created an abbreviation, MULE (Mammalia, Ungulata, Lack of functioning gonads, Eccentric). Due to the resulting population implosions, the research will terminate with the second generation of animals.

Experiments with Eggs for Shipping

Alexander Kohn

Holden has reported in *Worm Runner's Digest* (vol. 6, #2, p. 98, 1965) on the advantages of using square bananas for shipment. The basic treatment he describes for bananas may also be applied to eggs. The problem of shipping eggs is largely about efficient packing and preventing breakage. Eggs would be easier to handle if they were square rather than round. Squaring a circle has long been known to be quite difficult. But for eggs, simply multiplying eggs by eggs will result in square eggs.

$$E \times E = E^2$$

$$\bullet \times \bullet = \blacksquare$$

Such square eggs can be packed in units of four, nine, sixteen, twenty-five, etc., in simple cartons, and then shipped.

The next problem is what customers would do with square eggs. We advocate using a simple instrument that is well known to dentists. Supply each box with a root extractor, for use at the store. Using this instrument, the sellers would extract a root from the square eggs, and give the customer normal, round eggs.

A patent has been applied for.

Body Temperature of Pink Elephants

Deep rectal temperature of a pink Indian elephant is 37.7°C. This important information has been provided by B. H. Brattstrom, et al., of the Biology Department, Orange State College, Fullerton, California, published in the *Journal of Mammalogy* (1963, vol. 44, p. 282).

"We took advantage of the presence of 14 female Indian elephants, *Elephas maximus,* on the college campus for the First Intercollegiate Elephant Race, 11 May 1962, to record body temperatures of elephants of several sizes. . . . Elephants 1 and 2 were in the shade. Elephant 3 was covered with pink paint."

They compared deep rectal temperatures of five elephants, including the pink one, and suggested that young elephants may have higher body temperatures than adults.

A New Classification of Stones

M. J. Oppenheim, Hebrew University

T he classification is adaptable to all stones and should always be used.

The classification is both rigid and flexible. Concerning itself only with properties that can be either observed or inferred, it is truly scientific. Using this classification, a stone may be surely and swiftly identified, even at discovery.

A. There are three primary groups, based on provenance:
- Stones that have dropped down from Heaven form the first master group, hailstones. The Earth, lying as it does at the center of the Universe, has a peculiar tendency to attract all manner of such materials.
- Some stones, on the other hand, originate in the Underworld; they are later raised to the Earth's surface. These form the second master group, brimstones.

The products of volcanoes are their only undoubted representatives.

- Many stones have a purely terrestrial origin and aspect. These give the third and final master group, the tombstones.

B. Because it behooves the geologist to mark well the tectonic setting of his stones, tectonic considerations allow further subdivision into:

- Rolling stones: stones that have moved since formation.
- Corner stones: stones that have not moved since formation.

C. Physical properties allow the next categorization:

- Touch stones: stones that turn base metals into noble metals on stroking.
- Anti-touch stones: stones that do not turn base metals into noble metals even after much strenuous stroking.
- Lode stones: stones that, when placed on a cork floating in water, align themselves north–south.
- Anti-lode stones: stones that, when placed on a cork floating in water, do not align themselves north–south.

D. For accurate work it is recommended that the field relations of the stone be noted. These are

- The stone's color.
- The tone emitted by the stone when struck professionally with the hammer.

DESCRIPTION OF A ROCK USING THIS CLASSIFICATION

Abbreviations are not permitted because this would encourage slovenliness of habit and a cacophonous terminology. In describing a stone, the terms are to be used in the precisely opposite order to that given here.

Thus, a particular stone recently discovered by the author is correctly and completely described as an F sharp, brownish-yellow, anti-lode, touch corner tombstone.

THE RAKE'S PROGRESS, IN BIBLIOGRAPHICAL EPISODES, WITH FOOTNOTES
(NAMES OF ARTICLES OMITTED)

1. By Prof. A*

*Thanks are due to the Ignoble Research Foundation for a grant in support of work discussed in this paper; to my wife, without whom such work would in any case not have been possible; and also to my mother and father, for the same reasons. Miss Press prepared the manuscript from my notes with great ingenuity and also read the proofs. Mr. Z helped with the technical setup of the experiments, answering telephones, and doing various chores in both my lab and house. Both deserve my thanks, as well as those of the readers.

2. By Prof. A*

*In some of the experiments described in this paper I was helped by doctoral candidate Z, one of the young trainees in my department.

3. By Prof. A

[The name of Mr. Z does not appear in this publication. A discreet inquiry revealed that at about the date it was received, Z had submitted a thesis in which about half the results presented in this item were published. The readers will have to interpret this coincidence at their own discretion.]

4. By Prof. A and Dr. Z*

*This paper is based in part on the doctoral thesis of the junior author, prepared under the direction of the senior author.

5. By Dr. Z and Prof. A

6. By Dr. Z

[An inquiry showed that the omission of Prof. A's name in the customary footnote of thanks coincided with the professor's campaign to separate Z and his daughter, to terminate the affair bred by the footnote of item 1.]

7. By Dr. Z*

*My sincere thanks are due to my father-in-law, Prof. A.

8. By Prof. Z

9. A Handbook by Prof. Z*

*This handbook is dedicated to the memory of my late father-in-law and illustrious predecessor at this great institute, which, largely owing to his personal efforts as director, has succeeded in attracting a team of the most outstanding research scientists. All of these, too numerous to recount, deserve my thanks for their assistance in the work reported in the present volume, a work never before attempted.

Luxury auto body shop:
Mercedes Bent

The Ending

X. Perry Mental

Wrongly adjusted microphones help in losing the audience. This is especially true if there is only one microphone on the speaker's rostrum, and you happen to wander around while pointing to the screen or writing on the board. If you happen to have a neck or chest microphone, then a good method is to stand in front of the board with your back to the audience, and speak over your shoulder so that the microphone is well screened by your shoulders. If the people in the back rows are lip readers, they might understand what you are saying.

Now, most of the graphics are finished, most of the audience is nicely asleep, and you near the end of your lecture. An hour has gone, and you have barely managed to cover half of your material. You notice that your chairman is fidgeting and tries to catch your eye to indicate that you *must* end. You then say, "In conclusion I should like to say. . . ." This gives you five to ten minutes' grace. If you cannot end by then, say, "Finally, these results indicate . . .," which gives you another few minutes, and then you still may say, "To sum up. . . ."

There are speakers who, when warned by blinking lights or threatening posture of the chairman, put themselves at the mercy of the chairman and ask, "How much time do I have?," which does not give them much chance if the chairman is not a mouse. Some bolder types usually say, "If I still have 5 minutes, then . . ." and ignore the chairman.

Some intimidated speakers accelerate their delivery to a speed that permits only highly trained experts to keep track of the content.

It has been suggested that listeners should organize themselves in a Society for the Prevention of Cruelty to Listeners and present speakers with rules and regulations (and sanctions) *before* they start talking.

If .com became .con, these would be choice domains:

singsing.con

alcatraz.con

sanquentin.con

lubyanka.con

bastille.con

proand.con

spamphish.con

fidencegame.con

INVENTIONS THAT LIBERATE

Henry Winthrop, University of South Florida

- THE NO-WORK TEACHING MACHINE. This is aimed at making education thoroughly effortless. It turns its own handles, moves your wrist gently as you write answers, squeals with delight when your answers are correct, and exclaims "So what?" when they are wrong. This machine provides a bank of keys, any one of which, when pressed, will provide a plan for getting rid of your professor in case it, itself, fails to do so. Recommended by critics of education. Patent #4211843.

- ALL-PURPOSE WEIGHT REDUCER. This is a special liquid recommended for those who wish to lose weight rapidly. It possesses the following virtues: It dissolves your food, then dissolves your appetite, then dissolves your stomach, and finally dissolves your sanity. Guaranteed to give satisfaction in three days. If dissatisfied, your body will be returned, postage-free, no questions asked. Patent #2717477.

- THE DOUBLE-DUTY DOMESTIC HELPER. This mechanism attaches to the baby's crib to save time for fathers who are in a hurry to leave for work. Pressing a button makes it rediaper the baby and give father a shoeshine at the same time. When the machine works wrong (it happens!) it diapers father and gives the baby a shine. Patent #X1214612.

MORE MATHEMATICAL TERMS FOR SOCIAL DESCRIPTION

Henry Winthrop, University of South Florida

- **Level of confidence:** The degree to which you can trust what you hear–usually near zero.

- **Linear transformation:** How those who disagree are brought into line with what is good for everybody.

- **Möbius strip:** Any situation that the administration declares clearly does not have two sides.

- **Null hypothesis:** The recommended stance in interviewing candidates, by assuming they know nothing until they actually prove it.

- **Obtuse angle:** A foolish way of looking at a situation. Usually applied by staff and administration to one another's judgment.

"I'VE DECIDED TO LEAVE MY BODY TO SCIENCE."

The government is reporting that obesity is now this country's number one killer. A National Rifle Association spokesman said, "This is what we've been claiming all along: Guns don't kill people, bacon cheeseburgers kill people."

—Comedian Shaun Eli Breidbart, www.BrainChampagne.com

BOVINITY

William F. Jud

Geological animalies affect animal action. Cliffs, for example, make animals detour. Rivers make them swim. Subsurface structures align them. This latter fact permits geophysical evaluation of ore bodies.

A study has been initiated to determine alignment of cows, and the diurnal variations in the intensity and polarity of this alignment. It was found that in the morning, cows are generally aligned with their heads toward the pasture, and in the evening, just before sunset, their tails point in that direction. In addition, there is a definite drift and transport phenomenon in the direction of their heads. Flow lines are sharpest in all cases along the path leading to the barn, and are randomly spread in the pasture proper. The flux causing this alignment strengthens considerably below 15°C during a strong wind. The polar effect of wind is such that the cows are oriented with their tails toward the wind.

Bovinity flux was first recognized in the Missouri Ozarks. It is the custom there to graze stock over areas of underground mining. Because the original observations on diurnal alignment

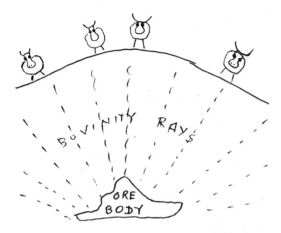

FIGURE 1: Sectional view of cows in spherical alignment in bovinity field emanating from buried ore body.

FIGURE 2: Cows in linear alignment in bovinity field radiating from recently active fault.

of cows were made in this locality, namely above ore bodies, it was desirable to verify this correlation in other localities.

Experiments performed in various geographic areas of known geologic structures, with cows of different breeds, showed an excellent correlation between the mining camp geology and bovine orientation, as shown in the figures.

Do you ever wonder how many

bugs there were before windshields?

—Doc Barham, www.DocBarham.com

Bird Buffet

Brian Malow, www.butseriously.com

On a road trip, I stopped at a rest area to use the facilities. When I came back I was surprised to find a bird eating bugs off the grill of my car.

I've seen this one other time, at a gas station, and in both cases it was clear that the bird had staked out the situation. It was not random luck that had provided this meal.

It was like evolution in progress. This bird has found his niche. He's figured out that he doesn't need to waste his time and energy hunting down bugs when a fresh shipment is coming in every few minutes!

A nice selection, still warm on the grill.

It's like a bird buffet: all you can eat!

We deliver!

What more do you want?

He probably thinks he has a symbiotic relationship with my car: "I get fed, you get groomed, everyone's a winner."

There should be published annual review articles in various fields under the titles of "Retreats in. . . ." For articles of a more general nature, we would offer *Recent Retrogressions*. A real bold step would be to publish *Retractions*. I am afraid, however, that such a journal would have many readers but perhaps no contributors. The scientific world may not be ready for it.

—E. A. Borger

A Brief History of Scholarly Publishing

Donald D. Jackson, University of Illinois Press

50,000 b.c.e. ○ Stone Age publisher demands that all manuscripts be double-spaced and hacked on one side of stone only.

1455 ○ Johannes Gutenberg applies to Ford Foundation for money to buy umlauts. First subsidized publishing venture.

1483 ○ Invention of ibid.

1507 ○ First use of circumlocution.

1859 ○ First use of "without whom" in acknowledgments.

1888 ○ Martyrdom of Ralph Thwaites, an author
who deletes 503 commas from his galleys
and is stoned by a copyeditor.

1897 ○ Famous old university press in England
announces that its Urdu dictionary has been
in print 400 years. Entire edition, accidentally
misplaced by a shipping clerk in 1497, is
found during quadricentennial inventory.

1901 ○ First free desk copy distributed (Black Thursday).

1916 ○ First successful divorce case based on failure
of author to thank his wife, in the foreword
of his book, for typing the manuscript.

1927 ○ Minor official in publishing house, who
suggests that his firm issue books in colorful
paper covers and market them through drug
houses, is passed over for promotion.

1928 ○ Early use of ambiguous rejection letter, beginning "While we have many good things to say about your manuscript, we feel that we are not now in a position. . . ."

1934 ○ Bookstore sends for two copies of Gleep's *Origin of Leases* from University Press and instead receives three copies of Darwin's *Storage of Fleeces,* plus half of a stale peanut butter sandwich from stockroom clerk's lunch. Beginning of a famous bookstore rebellion, resulting in temporary improvement in shipping practices.

1952 ○ Scholarly writing begins to pay: Professor Harley Biddle's publishing contract for royalties on his book after 1,000 copies have been sold to defray printing costs. Total sales: 1,009 copies.

1961 ○ Important case of *Dulany vs. McDaniel,* in which Judge Kelley rules that to call a doctoral dissertation a nonbook is libelous per se.

1962 ○ Copyeditors' anthem, "Revise or Delete," is first sung at national convention. Quarrel over hyphen in second stanza delays official acceptance.

Counter-ion

NOMEN OMEN:
BOOKS' AUTHORS AND SUBJECTS

Ball, A., *Ballistic and Guided Missiles*. Sportshelper Soccer Assn., 1960.

Cook, A. H., *Science of Barley and Malt.* Academic Press, 1962.

Cook, B., *More Fish to Fry.* Morrow, 1951.

Hunter, H., *Guns, Antique and Used Modern.* 3d ed. Follett, 1958.

Hunter, John A., *African Hunter.* Harper, 1954.

Hunter, John A., *Big Game Hunting in British East Africa.* Harper, 1952.

Goodenough, F. L., *Exceptional Children.* Appleton Century Crofts, 1956.

Goodspeed, J. M., *Let's Go to a Garage.* Putnam, 1957.

Slaughter, F. G., *In a Dark Garden.* Pocket, 1946.

REDUCING AUTOMOBILE ACCIDENTS

John L. S. Hickey

RECENTLY REPORTED RESEARCH BY the National Safety Program has provided a significant clue that, if properly exploited, can reduce and perhaps completely eliminate automobile accidents. The germ of the breakthrough lies in their finding that "75% of automobile accidents occur within 40 miles of home." Now, there are five ways in which one may react to this statement. Three are elementary:

1. NORMAL REACTION: "I should be just as vigilant driving near home as when on the highway."

2. STATISTICIAN'S REACTION: "Since about 90% of driving occurs within 40 miles of home, and only 75% of the accidents, this is a 'safe' area, and I can relax while driving."

3. REVERSE REACTION: "I'd better drive as fast as possible to get out of the 40-mile 'danger' zone into the surrounding 'safe' zone."

The fourth reaction is, "If 75% of accidents occur within 40 miles of home, the farther one is from home, the smaller the chance of an accident. Therefore, I will register my car at a 'home' 500 miles away and never go near there." This could easily spawn a national program to provide simulated or substitute homes for all drivers, perhaps titled Car Registration At Substitute Homes (CRASH).

The fifth reaction requires a little background. As we all know, accident rates vary from locality to locality; one can therefore expand on the fourth reaction and surmise that, instead of registering their car at a randomly chosen "home" 500 miles away, the safer thing to do would be to register it in a place much farther away that has a low automobile accident rate. A place immediately comes to mind: the South Pole. It is very far away, and there is only one automobile there, according to ads. Thus the automobile collision rate is necessarily zero, and cars registered in Antarctica will sustain this rate. Again, this concept could be expanded into a national program to register every car at the South Pole, named Central Location for Accident Prevention Through Registering Automobiles Polarilly (CLAPTRAP). Through this method, the automobile accident would become a thing of the past. The small risk? If another automobile were taken to Antarctica and collided with the first one, every car in the country would suddenly be registered in an area with a 100% accident rate.

FROM BANGHART, BACHRACH, AND
PATTISHALL, *STUDIES IN PROBLEM
SOLVING*, CONTRACT 474, OFFICE OF
NAVAL RESEARCH, SEPTEMBER 1959

"In other words, for this particular task, intelligence did not
seem to interfere with problem solving performance."

Love That Chocolate

Jim Eberhart,

University of Colorado at Colorado Springs

In a nonmajors chemistry class, I decided to share with my students something interesting I had read in a recent issue of *New Scientist* on the chemistry of chocolate. It seems that when we eat chocolate, MRI scans show that the same area of the brain is activated as during the initial phase of falling in love. So I passed this interesting news on to my chemistry class. One of my students raised her hand and asked in a very serious voice, "Doc, does that mean that chocolate is a good substitute for men?"

"WELL, DAD, HOW MANY MILLION GERMS DID YOU WIPE OUT TODAY?"

THE ERADICATION OF POVERTY IN CONTEMPORARY AMERICA

Alan Frankel, University of Portland

ABSTRACT: Without explicating specific psychological, social, political, and economic theories, and utilizing a hypothetico-deductive epistemology, a testable theorem is derived concerning the ontogenesis of poverty in contemporary America. A treatment strategy is suggested as well as a theory-related method of evaluation.

Poor people do not have enough money. Give them enough money. They will no longer be poor.

This study was financed in part by Grant No. RD 14-1063-7093/RPM-1049/ CIA/OSS/POOF from the Society for the Preservation of Social Sciences Interested in Nonparametric Hyper-Multivariate Research of Trivial Social Problems.

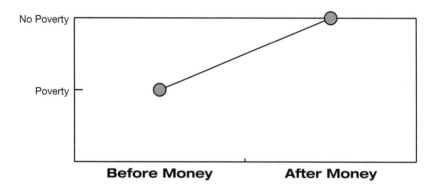

FIGURE 1: MATHEMATICAL REPRESENTATION OF THE
POVERTY-MONEY RELATIONSHIP, $r = 1.00$, $p < .0000001$

THE ETIOLOGY OF GRATEFUL PATIENT SYNDROME

Edith K. Peters

Grateful patient syndrome is one of the oldest known to man. Possibly the earliest roots were known to Neanderthal man, as exhibited by one caveman presenting another with a mastodon steak in return for being freed from a rock that crushed his foot.

It takes much more than gifts of food to keep today's medic solvent. He has taxes, insurance, registrations, and the Internal Revenue Service breathing down his neck. He enforces a schedule of fees, runs a tight ship, and tries to send his kids to college.

But still there is evidence of the syndrome. Given enough kinfolk, close friends, and business colleagues, a medic could wallow economically, were it not for the grateful patient. He checks the dentist's gall bladder and gets his children's teeth cleaned. He eases the psychosomatic mother of a car-selling friend through innumerable crises, and he gets a discount on his next horseless carriage.

That is right and fitting, but what of the grateful patient who can't estimate the cost of the service, won't try, and doesn't care? He feels he is entitled to a cut, so he returns the favor on a lesser plateau. Is the appendectomy worth only a pair of cuff links? Is the new baby worth only a magazine subscription? Of course, not everybody can present a matched set of golf clubs, a fitted doctor's bag, or a painting for the office, but it helps if some can.

During an epidemic there is commonly an onrush of duplicate desk lamps, paperweights, and medical textbooks. Too much of a good thing can be disastrous.

Successful management of the syndrome consists of guiding the grateful patient toward acute observation of the doctor's wants. This guarantees the medic a useful gift and enhances true thoughtfulness by the patient. It ranges from a season's snow removal or landscape service to swim fins and tennis balls. It is accomplished by urging care, patience, and sober consideration, guided not by economic resources but by a sincere desire to please. The syndrome is not fatal and can be rendered quite harmlessly acceptable.

Molybdenum can make some people act dyslexic, even in the absence of the molybdenum itself. All it takes is trying to *spell* the word.

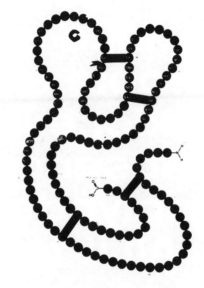

Lysozyme

The Molecular Theory of Management

Russel De Waard

It is interesting and informative to liken the growth and behavior of a company to that of a synthesized organic molecule. Take as an example polyvinyl chloride. In unplasticized form, this material is very hard, elastic, and brittle. There are many strong bonds between closely spaced charged atoms. When one adds diluent plasticizers, the bonds are weakened, as the inverse square law is invoked by the big putty-like molecules. The material becomes flexible, can absorb shock, and has commercial purposes: shower curtains, car window cranks, steering wheels, seat covers, and so on. These big molecules contribute to the modern economy of planned obsolescence. The molecules slowly lose their footing and leach out of your window crank, leaving behind a cracked handle at just about the same time as rust eats through your fenders.

241

A company also starts with a small group of charged particles. A lot of energy is produced, efficiency is high, and business is good. This nucleus rapidly acquires more particles. Because there is no time for careful screening, a large number of the big rubber-like molecules are added to the mix. Many other types of particles are admitted randomly. Their quality is inversely proportional to the management stature of the interviewer, and their salary is directly proportional. Unfortunately, many of the big molecules are completely inelastic diluents whose function appears to be to absorb the energy generated by the charged particles.

It is interesting to contrast these rubber-like additions to the neutrino of atomic physics: Whereas the latter has no charge and no mass, the former has no charge and is all mass.

If a growing company can avoid gathering too many of these particles, it can survive. If the converse holds, all the energy generated by the charged particles is absorbed by the diluents, and no energy or products can escape. Although the evidence pointing this way is sometimes strong, it is hard to believe that a company would consciously plan its own obsolescence.

GENETICS

Submitted by J. Gressel

INSTRUCTIONS: No cheating, peeking, or grade.

1. Mitosis is:
    A. Those funny-looking things at the end of my feet
    B. My sister's baseball glove
    C. The janitor who cleans up the lab

2. Anaphase is:
    A. A girl friend of mitosis
    B. A girl with an ugly phase
    C. A mother of invention

3. Meiosis is:
    A. Sis's noisy cat
    B. Chairman Mao's sister
    C. A half-breed mitosis

4. If we cross a blue-eyed female with a brown-eyed male, they will:
    A. Be uncomfortable
    B. Flunk the course
    C. Not give a hoot

5. Genes are:
    A. A group of men called Eugene
    B. A group of little cells called Eugene
    C. DeNAtured threads

6. If we breed 200 male flies and 100 female flies, we can infer that they will:
    A. Itch like the dickens
    B. Have romantic triangles
    C. Need a fly swatter

The Second Law

Jim Eberhart,

University of Colorado at Colorado Springs

Usually the grading of final exams is pretty grim stuff. But a few years ago my physical chemistry finals were an exception. One of my questions asked the students to state the Second Law of Thermodynamics. During the semester they had learned that processes have a natural direction and that, in an isolated system, natural processes are always accompanied by an increase in entropy. My most creative student had a version that delighted me and made the grading process truly memorable. He wrote, "You can't stuff road apples up a horse's behind and get oats out of his mouth." That statement pretty much sums up the directionality of natural processes.

The Journal of Irreproducible Results asks subscribers what they collect.
Less serious responses include the following:

- my wits
- dust
- bills
- debts
- junk
- blunders
- smashed pennies
- credit card offers
- experiences
- old husbands
- memories that embarrass other people
- dead computer parts
- things old, dirty, junky, rusty, and handmade
- magazines that should be thrown out
- neutrinos
- zeros
- null sets

Hydroxyproline

FROM A. S. PARKES, "THE ART OF SCIENTIFIC DISCOVERY," *PERSPECTIVES IN BIOLOGY AND MEDICINE*, 1958, 7, 366

"It has often been pointed out that a very good example of the use of hypothesis is provided by Columbus's discovery of America; it has many features of a classic discovery in science. Columbus was obsessed with the idea that if the Earth were round, he could reach the East Indies by sailing west.

Notice:

a. The idea was by no means original, but he had obtained some additional scraps of information.

b. He met great difficulties in getting someone to provide the money as well as making the actual experiment.

c. He did not find the expected new route, but instead, found a new half of the world.

d. Despite all evidence to the contrary, he clung to the belief that he had found a new route to the Orient.

e. He got little credit or reward during his lifetime.

f. Evidence has since been brought forward that he was by no means the first European to reach America."

MORE

MATHEMATICAL TERMS FOR SOCIAL DESCRIPTION

Henry Winthrop, University of South Florida

- **Partial derivative:** Any professor's offspring of questionable fatherhood.

- **Partially ordered scale:** Faculty salaries that bear little relation to ability and merit.

- **Permutation:** One of a large number of ways to express the same threadbare idea to fill up space in a report.

- **Phase operator:** Someone you can count on to embarrass the enemy.

- **Radical:** Faculty members who try to get at the root of things.

Meyer's Variable Constant

J. L. Meyer, MD

Some years ago I worked out a basic concept for finding quick statistics. I cannot claim priority, for my work was too embryonic, and the only published material was in a letter to the editor of a midwestern weekly.

I called my discovery Meyer's Variable Constant, and my first derivation was obtained by adding together all the data in a problem from my college math book and dividing it by the answer in the back of the book.

I'm sure others have far surpassed my sophistication. But when you are unsinging heroes, perhaps you will unsing a brief chorus for me. The Variable Constant, I need not add, is irreproducible from one problem to the next and disappears completely if there is no answer section in the book.

Kohn's Second Law:
AN EXPERIMENT IS REPRODUCIBLE UNTIL ANOTHER LABORATORY TRIES TO REPEAT IT.

Bernstein's Law:
A FALLING BODY ALWAYS ROLLS TO THE MOST INACCESSIBLE SPOT.

McGurk's Law:
AN IMPROBABLE EVENT THAT WOULD CREATE MAXIMUM CONFUSION IF IT DID OCCUR, WILL OCCUR.

FROM "DEVELOPMENT OF EDUCATIONAL
THEORY DERIVED FROM THREE
EDUCATIONAL THEORY MODELS,"
BY ELIZABETH S. MACCIA AND
GEORGE S. MACCIA, U.S. OFFICE
OF EDUCATION PROJECT #5-0683,
CONTRACT #OE 4-10-186

p. 49: "Toputness is system environmentness."

p. 50: "Storeputness is a system with inputness that is
not fromputness."

p. 55: "Disconnectionness is not either complete
connectionness or strongness or unilateralness
or weakness and some components are not
connected with respect to affect relations."

p. 56: "Passive dependentness is components which
have channels to them."

p. 57: "Segretationness is independentness under system environmental changeness."

p. 63: "Size growthness is increase in sizeness."

p. 66: "Stressness is change beyond certain limits of negasystem state."

p. 67: "Strainness is change beyond certain limits of system state."

p. 98: "[The basic information properties of a system] are toputness, inputness, storeputness, feedinness, feedoutness while those of a negasystem are fromputness and outputness."

p. 98: "Only the condition of selectivity is needed to give meaning to toputness, inputness, fromputness and outputness."

p. 100: "In other words, feedinness is the shared information between toputness and inputness, where the toputness is at a time just prior to the inputness."

p. 150: "If school resource increases and school storage is greater than some value, then (this leads to) school segretationness with respect to referent affect relation."

p. 192: "The development of the educational theory from set theory (s), information theory (I), graph theory (G), and general systems theory (GS) integrated into the SIGGS Theory Model has set the stage for survival."

Isoleucine

A Biological Study of Pool Life

S. Flowers

A rich variety of wild life has appeared in the habitat of the swimming pool in an amazingly short time. Among the many new species, the following have been observed:

- Hippopotami (Hippopotamidæ) are those that puff and pant as they swim around clumsily.
- Elephants (Elephantidæ) are those that trumpet and spout water over anyone within range.
- Turtles (Chelonia), slow and sure, do their daily kilometer or more.
- Seals (Phocidæ) swim gracefully and effortlessly, their sleek heads breaking the smooth surface only for air, and they are capable of covering vast distances.
- Tadpoles (Ramidæ) are these plump, bright-eyed little creatures that flash in and out of the paddling pool. It is usual to find a croaking frog or ungainly stork in the vicinity.

- Porpoises (Odontoceti) are easily recognized. They resemble children as they frolic and splash all over the place.
- Pool lizards (Lacertidæ) are the languorous dark creatures seen stretched out around the pool. They are usually the female of the species. A noted anthropologist informed me that this is perhaps because the males of the species are too busy studying the few perfect female specimens and are therefore more likely to be found slithering in and out of the pool.

Vide Infra

Dr. Tim Healey

As a keen[1] student[2] of footnotes,[4] I have long[14]

---

1. Enthusiastic, not necessarily sharp.[13]

2. When the late Dr. John Wilkie[18] stood up and said, "As a mere student in these matters . . .," the listeners knew that they were about to hear some words of wisdom from a very experienced expert.[16,24] Modesty[17a] forbids me to draw a parallel.

3. Blaise[17b] Pascal used the same trick with his phrase, "It is easy to show that . . ." Experienced mathematicians soon recognized that these words warned them that the next step would take them three days of complex calculations to understand.

4. I have been fascinated by footnotes ever since I obtained several editions of a book[5] that has some of the best footnotes[6] I have ever encountered.[7]

5. Samson Wright's *Applied Physiology.*[8]

6. E.g. text: "Never occurs." Footnote: "What, never? Well, hardly ever."

7. A book called *Useless Facts in History* has a good pair[9] also.

8. The footnotes disappeared after the ninth edition, when Samson Wright died. His major work has been continued,[10] but the footnotes that gave it individuality are no longer given—a grave mistake.

9. There are only two in the book.[11]

10. Tenth edition by C. A. Keele and E. Neil, O.U.P., London, 1961.

11. The first says, "Do you like footnotes?" The second says, "Aha![12] Caught you again."

12. Note the similar style to Lucy.[15]

13. Though I do not deny it.

14. There is no room for the rest of this article because my allotted space is entirely taken up with footnotes. However, I was merely going to state that it has been my ambition to write an article wholly composed of footnotes.[20] My resolve weakened, and I included a first line.

15. In the *Peanuts* cartoon strip by Schulz[24] in the *Daily Sketch.*[19]

16. He was never wrong.[6]

17. This juxtaposition no doubt reflects my admiration for the work of Mr. Peter O'Donnell.

18. Of Sheffield.

19. Now defunct. The *Sketch* and the strip have gone to the *Mail*.

20. Footnotes should not be confused with references. Thus, [10] is a footnote, not a reference. References have a special charm of their own. I cherish a reprint of an article describing one case, with seven alleged co-authors and seventy-three references. Famous physics papers include those by Bhang and Gunn; Alpher, Bethe, and Gamow; and Sowiski and Soda. In my capacity as science editor for an international journal, I get not a few crank papers for assessment. I have learned to recognize these at a glance by the facts that a) the references always come first, and b) the list includes (always at number 5 or 6, for some unknown reason) "5: 'Some inane observations on

some perfectly well worked out phenomena' by N.A.D.[21] Six copies, privately circulated, six years ago."

21. The author of the paper being considered. They always use only initials here.

22. You will observe that not all footnotes are brief. A recent article[23] I wrote was originally subtitled "A Footnote to History." It occupied two sides of news-sheet with 3,000 words. The subeditorial pencil removed the subtitle, but a comment on the article in *People* restored my faith in the subeditorial class. This genius[24] dreamed up the heading "Queen of Drag."

23. "Was the Virgin Queen a Man?" *Pulse,* September 1971.

24. Credit where credit is due.

Real Exam Answers from
Earth Science Students

Brenna Lorenz, Penn State University

- The terrestrial planets are much larger than the gas giants.
- Wegener found matching bedbugs on opposite sides of the Atlantic.
- The main problem associated with limestone aquifers is Lyme disease.
- We don't have rock salt on Guam because that forms from evaporation of oceans, and we don't have oceans on Guam.
- Erie, Pennsylvania, has no volcanoes because it's too cold there.
- The most important agent of landscape formation on Guam is greyhounds; they are intelligent.
- We know that the Sun is much farther away from us than the Moon is because we can see stars between us and the Sun but not between us and the Moon.
- The rear end of a trilobite is called a trilobutt.

PAEAN TO A STOP PLOSIVE ─────────

C. W. Fuller

In the search for perfect diction,
For speech that is ultra-fine,
A critical question arises:
"Does your /p/ sound seem like mine?"

An issue implied in this question
Is one that we wish to forestall;
We will not discuss whether /p/ sounds
Ever sound seemly at all.

Instead we would shout "Hallelujah"
To distillers of phonemic mash
Who choose the ubiquitous /p/ sound
With which to make a big splash.

The grossly inaccurate /p/ sound
Is one we can hardly commend,
But the /p/ that is right on the target
Is easy for us to defend.

O Shanks doesn't smoke marijuana
Nor freak out by LSD-ing;
When pressure becomes overwhelming,
He relaxes himself by /p/-ing.

So compare your skills with this model
Of a speech pathology whiz;
You can rest assured of your future
If your /p/ sound seems like his.

Science in general can be considered a technique with which fallible people try to outwit their own human propensities to fear the truth, to avoid it, to distort it.

—A. H. Maslow, *The Psychology of Science,* 1966, p. 29

If .org became .arg, these would be choice domains:

irs.arg

fired.arg

lost.arg

crash.arg

brokeit.arg

pirates.arg

breakup.arg

missedit.arg

MINIFLY RESEARCH SUGGESTS
SOLUTION TO OVERCROWDING

To the delight of miniaturization experts, researchers have found a way to make tiny fruit flies even smaller.

An injection of minimine, a toxic polypeptide isolated from bee venom, into fruit fly larvæ results in a ¼-size adult.

The miniflies are normal in every way except that their individual cells are miniature. The new breed have a normal lifespan and produce regular-size offspring.

The implications for city planners, doomsday prophets, and zero population growth zealots are staggering. Minimine injections into human embryos might produce a ¼-size human. That would solve many of the world's overpopulation problems.

Consuming only 25% of the current living space and food, the minipeople density could total four times the current population before reaching today's wretched state. The production of miniature housing, tools, appliances, and other necessities would produce an unprecedented economic boom. Present common carriers could quadruple their capacity at no additional cost, and even the narrowest two-lane rural roads would become four-lane superhighways for new miniautos.

Admittedly, the first few generations would have difficulty with leftover awkward, lumbering giants of an earlier age, but room soon would become available for them to live out their last few years.

Separating the Chaff

F. C. Martin

*C**haff* is a term familiar to anyone in electronic warfare. Developed during World War II, it consists of large numbers of very-light-weight strips of conducting material, designed to be ejected from an aircraft and float very slowly to the ground. As long as the chaff is high enough, it strongly reflects energy from enemy radars, confusing the radar operators.

Naturally, the longer it takes to sink to the ground, the more effective it is. The relationship between persistence and effectiveness was formulated in 1966 by Francis C. Martin, an electronic engineer at Cornell Aeronautical Laboratory in Buffalo. In its most compact form, "Martin's Conjecture" states, "He whose chaff lasts chaffs best."

FROM N. S. KLINE, "YOU CAN'T GET THERE FROM HERE," *INDIAN JOURNAL OF PSYCHIATRY*, 1959, 1, 118–125

"Perhaps someone should set up a foundation for the support of Improbable and Fantastic Ideas since these are frequently the area in which new and important advances are to be made. One qualification for grants-in-aid to such an Institute might be that they must have been rejected by at least 2 of the more respectable fund-giving sources."

ERRATA

Jef Raskin

Due to circumstances in our control, the following bibliography was not omitted from Professor Raskin's article "General Systemic Applications of Computer Systems" that was not published in this journal two numbers back. Since then it has been called to our attention, and we do not regret having not omitted it at that time. Nonetheless, in fairness to the author, we will publish it here and do not apologize for the lack of inconvenience it has caused our readers.

1. J. Wentworth Knox. "A Direct Hardware Simulation of Peristalsis on an IBM 360/65." *J. Bio. Phys. Res.,* 19(8).

2. Edward Saachen, Jr., Ed., "Programming at 137 Hierarchical Levels Above Machine Language," *Comm. Comp. Soc. Am.,* 8(3).

3. Joshi Swadalahari, "A Sanskrit–Russian Translator Written in J.C.L.," *Comm. Comp. Soc. Am.,* 6(11).

4. Albert M. Sooth, "A General Algorithm for Computer Problems in the Social Sciences," *Lib. Arts Rev. Comp. Appl.,* June 1972.

5. Janislaus Stanislaw, "The Problems of Early Dyadic Notation as Employed by Three Monks of the Clausian Order in 1436," *Comp. in the Universe,* 9(6).

6. Henry Balzeau, "Trivial Applications of the Computer in Three Significant Areas" (French), *Rev. Fran. Fed. Comp.,* 4, 3336–3422.

7. Francis Label, "Finding the Theme of the First Movement of Beethoven's Fifth Symphony on the IBM 1401/1403 Computer System," *Comp. Mus. Abstracts,* 1(1).

8. J. C. Godde and Floyd Schweppes, "Organizing a Summer Institute in Computer Applications in Unwarranted Disciplines: An Omniscient Overview," *Comp. Ed. Soc. Am.,* 3(4).

9. Jane Sotentia, "A Substantive Analysis of Synthetic Constructs," *J. Comp. Phil. Int.,* 9, 102.

10. J. Handex, Michael R. Barr, Lincoln Soamy, R. M. Vinograd, Selma Florien, and John Scarpe, "A.C.A.I. Instruction Method for Teaching Teachers to Compile Compilers for Computer Assisted Instruction of Teachers," *Comp. Ed. Soc. Am.,* 2(22).

11. Carnot Jeckl, "The Man–Machine Relationship in Shakespeare's *Twelfth Night,*" *J. Eng. Lit.,* 193(6).

12. Philip McCarthy, "An Application of Optical Character Recognition to Finding Capital Letters in 19th Century Prose," *Comm. Comp. Soc. Am.,* 6(11).

13. Samuel Orangethorpe, "On the Possibilities of Using Natural Language as a Human Communication Medium," *Bull. Ed. Soc. Am.,* 3(1).

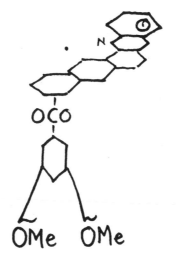

Reserpine

WHAT WAS THAT? ———————————

Jack McCarthy

> There is sometimes security
> In well-contrived obscurity.
> If words are large
> And most abstract
> And preferably
> Quite densely packed,
> Then you can claim
> That they are dense
> Because they do
> Not see the sense.

Ten Commandments for the Project Manager

B. Sparks, Consulting Engineer

1. Strive to look tremendously important.

2. Attempt to be seen with important people.

3. Speak with authority, but expound only on the obvious and proven facts.

4. Don't engage in arguments, but if cornered, ask an irrelevant question and lean back with a satisfied grin while your opponent tries to figure out what's going on, then quickly change the subject.

5. Listen intently while others are arguing the problem. Pounce on a trite statement and bury them with it.

6. If a subordinate asks you a pertinent question, look at him as if he had lost his senses. When he looks down, paraphrase the question back at him.

7. Obtain a brilliant assistant, but keep him out of sight and out of the limelight.

8. Walk fast when out of the office; this keeps questions from subordinates and superiors to a minimum.

9. Always keep the office door closed; this puts visitors on the defensive and also makes it look as if you are always in important conferences.

10. Give all orders orally. Never write anything down that might go into a "disaster file."

Acetic Acid

MORE

MATHEMATICAL TERMS FOR SOCIAL DESCRIPTION

Henry Winthrop, University of South Florida

- **Random walk:** When you go from one official to another without accomplishing anything.

- **Rank-order coefficient:** A measure of the status of staff members, usually directly proportional to their point of inflection.

- **Saddle point:** A lull in a meeting when nonsense from the speaker reaches a maximum, and enthusiasm of the audience reaches a minimum.

- **Second-order infinitesimal:** The annual improvement in teachers' salaries voted by some state legislators.

- **Skewness:** A character disorder that shifts one's position left or right, depending where the advantage is.

St. Louis Cardinals:
"We're Number One!"

St. Louis Ordinals:
"We're in First Place!"

STANDARD PROGRESS REPORT FOR ANY PROJECT THAT HAS NO PROGRESS

B. Sparks, Consulting Engineer

The report period just ended has seen considerable progress in directing a large portion of the effort in meeting the initial objectives established.[1] Additional background information and relevant data have been acquired to assist in problem resolution.[2] As a result, some realignment has been made to enhance the position of the project.[3]

One deterrent that has caused considerable difficulty in this reporting period was the selection of optimum methods and techniques. However, this problem is being vigorously attacked, and we expect the development phase will proceed at a satisfactory rate.[4] In order to prevent unnecessary duplication of previous efforts in the same field, it was deemed necessary to establish a special team to conduct a survey of facilities engaged in similar activities.[5]

The Project Control Group held its regular meeting and considered the broad functional aspects of all levels of coordination and cross-fertilization of relevant ideas associated with the general specifications of the evolving system.[6] At the present rate of progress, it is believed that most project milestones will be met.[7] During the next quarter, a major breakthrough is anticipated and will be fully covered in the next progress report.[8]

1. The project has long ago forgotten what the objective was.
2. The one page of data from the last quarter was found in the incinerator.
3. We now have a new leader for the data group.
4. We finally found some information that is relevant to the project.
5. We had a great time in Los Angeles, Denver, and New York.
6. Fertilizer.
7. Would you be happy with one or two?
8. We think we have stumbled onto someone who knows what's going on.

Notices About Absenteeism

Submitted by N. V. B. Manyam, MD

Surgery: We wish to discourage any thoughts that you may need an operation, as we believe that as long as you are an employee here, you will need all of whatever you have, and you should not consider having anything removed. We hired you as you are, and to have anything less would certainly make you less than we bargained for.

Death (your own): This will be accepted as an excuse, but we would like to have two weeks' notice.

Uracil

The Journal of Irreproducible Results has been entertaining scientists, doctors, engineers, and educators since 1955, when Alexander Kohn and Harry J. Lipkin founded it in Israel. Spoofs target verbose scientists, shortsighted decision makers, and pseudoscientific distortions. Check www.jir.com for articles, subscriptions, and enrichment.

Norman Sperling began subscribing and contributing articles to *JIR* in the 1970s while directing a planetarium, and became editor in 2004. He teaches freshman astronomy for the University of California at Berkeley.